चिन्मय ग्रन्थ माला

parables

Swami Chinmayananda

Central Chinmaya Mission Trust

•

First Edition - 1981 - 5,000 copies
Printed upto - November 2011 - 28,000 copies
Second Edition - September 2014 - 2,000 copies

•

Published by:
Chinmaya Prakashan
The Publications Division of
Central Chinmaya Mission Trust
Sandeepany Sadhanalaya
Saki Vihar Road, Powai, Mumbai 400072, India
Tel.: +91-22-2857 2367, 2857 5806 Fax: +91-22-2857 3065
Email: ccmtpublications@chinmayamission.com
Website: www.chinmayamission.com

•

Distribution Centre in USA:
Chinmaya Mission West
Publications Division
560 Bridgetown Pike Langhorne, PA 19053, USA
Tel.: 1-888-CMW-READ, (215) 396-0390 Fax: (215) 396-9710
Email: publications@chinmayamission.org
Website: www.chinmayapublications.org

•

Designed by:
Chinmaya Kalpanam, Mumbai

•

Printed by:
Usha Multigraphics Pvt. Ltd., Mumbai - 400 013, Tel.: 2492 5354

•

Price: ₹ 75/–

•

ISBN 978-81-7597-655-9

Transliteration and Pronunciation Guide

In the book, Devanāgarī characters are transliterated according to the scheme adopted by the International Congress of Orientalists at Athens in 1912. In it one fixed pronunciation value is given to each letter; f, q, w, x and z are not called to use. An audio recording of this guide is available at http://chinmayamission.com/scriptures.php. According to this scheme:

Devanāgarī	Transliteration	Sounds Like	Devanāgarī	Transliteration	Sounds Like
अ	a	son	द्	ḍh	adhesive*
आ	ā	father	ण्	ṇ	under*
इ	i	different	त्	t	tabla
ई	ī	feel	थ्	th	thumb
उ	u	full	द्	d	this
ऊ	ū	boot	ध्	dh	Gandhi
ऋ	ṛ	rhythm*	न्	n	nose
ॠ	ṝ	**	प्	p	pen
ऌ	ḷ	**	फ्	ph	phantom*
ए	e	evade	ब्	b	boil
ऐ	ai	delight	भ्	bh	abhor
ओ	o	core	म्	m	mind
औ	au	now	य्	y	yes
क्	k	calm	र्	r	right
ख्	kh	khan	ल्	l	love
ग्	g	gate	व्	v	very
घ्	gh	ghost	श्	ś	shut
ङ्	ṅ	ankle*	ष्	ṣ	sugar
च्	c	chuckle	स्	s	simple
छ्	ch	witch*	ह्	h	happy
ज्	j	justice	ं	ṁ	improvise
झ्	jh	Jhansi	ः	ḥ	**
ञ्	ñ	banyan	क्ष्	kṣ	action
ट्	ṭ	tank	त्र्	tr	three*
ठ्	ṭh	**	ज्ञ्	jñ	gnosis
ड्	ḍ	dog	ऽ	'	a silent 'a'

* These letters don't have an exact English equivalent. An approximation is given here.
** These sounds cannot be approximated in English words.

We take the opportunity to thank our donors
for having sponsored the printing of this book
and ensuring that this timeless wisdom
reaches the hands of seekers galore.

Contents

Contents

Preface

None of these stories that are attributed to me are really mine. These are stories that the old Mahātmās had told us while we were learning the scriptures at Rishikesh and Uttarkashi.

This is an old method - an intelligent application of audio-visual method of education for imparting knowledge of Vedānta. The ideas expounded in Vedānta are extremely subjective and therefore supremely subtle. Chances of misunderstanding or vaguely understanding are more than that of true understanding or right comprehension. As a methodology in communication of scriptural knowledge, our ancient Masters found that examples given from the gross outer world can perhaps correctly illumine the subtle inflections in the sensitive march of ideas in Vedānta.

Do not take these stories literally and apply them to the entire idea or concept each claims to illumine; no example or story can do this. The finite can never illustrate or totally bring into the vivid comprehension of the limited intellect the Supreme, the Infinite. Our equipments are limited; language cannot but stammer in its despairing limitation to express the beauty of all beauties. These parables can bring out in all brilliance the total light in each one of the great jewels of Vedānta. Those of you who read each one of them can give sufficient thought to its implication

Parables

and can be benefited greatly in gaining a clearer glimpse into the subtle imports that are intelligently suggested by the pregnant mantras of the Upaniṣads and the galloping stanzas of the *Bhagavad-gītā*.

Bangalore
15.12.80   **Swami Chinmayananda**

1. The V. I. P.

Arantangi, a tiny town in the district of Dharia, was unusually busy. The usual quiet and calmness of the place had given place to din and bustle with the honking and hooting of dubious contraptions lumbering along the road. A trail of dust intermittently ascending to the welkin marked the progress of the day. The town was preparing itself to go to the polls. Many were the contestants. Thatched structures had already made their appearance on important roads. Those were the offices of the contesting politicians' vassals. Tea and coffee flowed freely in these hutments. Each structure was decorated with festoons of party flags. Urchins crowded the place, watching their elders indulging in the mugs game. In the morning, in the centre of the road, temporary platforms were built for contesting politicians to indulge in the game of mud-slinging and vituperative attack on their opponents. These were the structures where, through harangues, dirty linen was washed. The motley throng enjoyed such emotional outbursts and got entertainment after their hard day's labour. This motley throng, in their unsophisticated naivete, felt that no one candidate was better than the other. The contestants too, to whatever party they belonged, indulged in tall promises. Manifestos were there for each party, but in the hustings, they did not manifest.

Ramachandran was an ordinary citizen of Arantangi. He came from humble beginnings. Even while at school, studying in the 10th Standard, he rarely studied the prescribed textbooks. With gusto and avidity he used to participate in all the strikes and bandhas. His teachers often used to tell him that he would shine well as a politician. Ramachandran left school without taking his examination. The call of politics was stronger than the call for studies. From then on, becoming a four anna member of the party in power, he learnt all the gimmicks of the party men. He went up the ladder in party politics, playing second fiddle to the leaders in power, pandering to those with money and power. Soon he learnt to play ducks and drakes with the easy money he earned. He learnt to talk at the top of his voice and browbeat others in conversation and debate.

Years rolled by. Soon he found himself being favoured by the party bosses with a party ticket for the elections to the Parliament. So here he was, in the din and bustle of Arantangi, actively campaigning for his own candidature. With words of learned length and thundering sound, punctuated often with trite truisms, he amazed the gazing motley crowd ranged around him. To his amazement he found himself defeating his nearest rival by 9787 votes! At last his dreams had come true! He could go to the Lok Sabha with full honours. He had become a full-fledged Member of Parliament, clad in the loose white kurta and a flowing white dhoti that swept the streets; he presented a picture of a seasoned politician.

That year the first session of Parliament was in progress in Delhi. Ramachandran, who could not contain his joy at his unbounded success, wanted to make himself known in his locality. So he sent a cable to his followers in Arantangi thus, 'Arriving there on the 26th. Arrange an inauguration or an opening ceremony'. It was his wish that his followers should arrange for him a grand function where he would be able to inaugurate an enterprise or perform an opening ceremony. He left the details of the arrangements to his followers. The followers too, wishing to please their leader, went about looking for a place or a project that needed inauguration. They were at their wit's end, for nothing had been left unturned in Arantangi by their leader predecessors in politics. The schools were opened, the cottage industries were opened, the shops were opened, the choultries were opened, houses too had been opened, nay, even the gutters opened, nay, even the housetops and roofs were opened. Nothing was left unopened or not inaugurated. The followers moved hither and thither, meeting this man and that man, trying to find out if something could be done to satisfy the vanity of their leader.

On one of their rounds they came across an elementary school teacher who was a jack of all trades. This teacher asked them, "Hey you fellows, why do you move about with woebegone and careworn faces? What has happened to you? What ails you?" The followers explained to the teacher their predicament. The teacher, with a twinkle in his eyes, said, "So, that is the problem. You want to arrange an inauguration. Leave everything to me and rest content. I shall arrange such a function. Do not worry". But they said, "Masterjī, what is there not yet inaugurated? Is there really anything which we have failed to notice?" The master, flaunting a broad smile, said, "Look here, you have unburdened your problem to me and now it is my concern. I told you I would arrange everything for you. I am a man who keeps his word. Have trust in me. Go and send a telegram to your leader saying that you have arranged for an inauguration and that he can come. Do not ask me the details now. In time you will come to know them. Give me a hundred rupees to go about with the work. In the meanwhile you start erecting a dais in the maidan, on the right side of the Śiva temple. Invite all the gentry of the town and the bigwigs from the surrounding villages". The followers having sent the telegram, went about arranging for the grand function.

The eventful day arrived. Yet the party followers were unable to wheedle out from the local teacher what exactly was to be inaugurated. The teacher was tight-lipped and reticent in this matter. The Member of Parliament arrived. He was given a V.I.P. reception at the station. Tabors, pipes, timbrels and cymbals produced notes of wild ecstasy, and amidst the tunes of the nādasvaram, the V.I.P. asked his followers in a whisper, "Hey, tell me quickly, what am I going to inaugurate or open? You have kept me in the dark about this all these days. I need to know now, for I have to marshal my thoughts before I make a speech at the function." Wringing their hands in anxiety the followers said, "Sir, everything has been arranged. But we too, have been kept in the dark about what you are to inaugurate, though there is certainly something for you to inaugurate. The local teacher is the one who is organising it. He refused to divulge it to us. Perhaps he wants to spring a surprise for you."

They searched for the teacher. But by the time they could seek him out, they were hustled to the dais. The moment the V.I.P. came to the dais, the programme was started. The prayer was sung by a tiny tot. Then the teacher emerged and requested the V.I.P. to come down to perform the inauguration. The V.I.P. who was on pins and needles to know what he was to inaugurate, followed the teacher who led him out of the place quickly. He headed towards the river, hopping from rock to rock. The V.I.P. had to hurry to keep pace with the teacher. When they reached the step touching the water of the river, the teacher gave the V.I.P. a silver tumbler and asked him to fetch water in the tumbler. When the V.I.P. had done so, the teacher asked him to lift it over his head and pour the water in the river. Then, retrieving the silver tumbler from the V.I.P. he asked him to come up with him to the dais. The V.I.P. was at sixes and sevens, for he knew not what all this meant. The teacher, by this time, had brought the V.I.P. to the dais. Going upto the microphone, the teacher started addressing the gathering.

"Ladies and gentlemen, you have all witnessed the solemn function of the inauguration of the river by our august Member of Parliament, Śrī Ramachandran. Today is a red letter day in the annals of our town's history. It is really kind and considerate of our esteemed Member of Parliament to have condescended to grace this occasion with his mighty presence inspite of his multifarious activities and inaugurate the river of our town. He has rightly declared it open. We, the residents and citizens of this town, are much beholden to him for this kind gesture of his. Let us offer our deep sense of gratitude to our Member of Parliament".

Here, the teacher took the garland that was in the basket and garlanded the Member of Parliament and clapped his hands. All took the cue and clapped their hands. The Member of Parliament was beside himself in ecstasy. He stood up, spoke some sentences and sat down. The function concluded. Not a soul there divined the joke the teacher had played on the V.I.P.

On this tumultuous planet of ours, are we not also foolishly acting like the V.I.P. who thought he was inaugurating the ever perennial river which had been flowing there from time immemorial? The very same river had given life to the V.I.P.'s forefathers. The very V.I.P. had many a times, spent his languorous boyhood days on the very banks of the river. As an urchin, had he not learnt swimming in this very river? Now, swollen-headed, he had the temerity to say that he had inaugurated the river.

In fact no undertaking is a new act that has an independent beginning or an end. All actions in the world are in an eternal pattern of the total world movements. If correctly analysed, our undertakings are controlled, regulated, governed and ordered by the available world of things and situations. Apart from them all, no independent action is undertaken or can be fulfilled by anyone. We should be conscious of this fact and not work in the world as an independent agent in the undertaking. The one inaugurator is the Lord. He inaugurated this cycle of creation and set it in motion and we should recognise that all our undertakings are mere links in that great chain of actions coming from the immemorial past into the immediate present and flowing into the infinite future.

2. The Cook and The King

Ranti Deva was the matchless king of the mighty Krīḍāpura Deśa. Endowed with a golden heart that flowed with the milk of human kindness, this king ruled over his subjects with a sense of justice, tempered with mercy. It was a land of milk and honey, pearls and rubies, peace and contentment. The king too paid meet adoration to the household gods and showed due care and concern in the proper worship of the deities in the temples of his land. Religious by nature and being charitably disposed, Ranti Deva always had the welfare of his subjects uppermost in his heart. Tutored in the disciplines of the spirit, he strove to subdue his lower self by gaining the knowledge of the higher. With an attitude of surrender unto the Lord of his heart, he carried on his regal duties, ever conscious that the Lord was the One who was sporting through him. This good and noble king was blessed with an equally noble and pious man as a minister. Ever conscious of the benign presence of the supreme Lord, the Jagadīśvara, this minister went about his duties seeing in all happenings, good or bad, the hand of God. And the name of God was ever on his lips.

Time sports and takes its toll. Golden lads and girls all must, as chimney sweeps, come to dust. The king too, breathed his last. The crown prince, the king's son, ascended the throne. The pious minister continued with his task as the adviser to the new king. This new king, Hemacūḍa Deva, though endowed with a mental calibre of a high order, was prone to bouts of pride and spasms of vanity. As a rose to a thorn, so was the pious minister for the new king. The king felt that the minister was a thorn in his path as the minister was often referring to the will of God. Hemacūḍa Deva did not like this. Once or twice, he even hinted to the minister of his displeasure. Yet the minister pretended not to understand the king. This attitude of the minister irritated the king all the more.

Once, after a court convention, the king, accompanied by his minister, was coming down a flight of steps when suddenly he tripped, tumbled down and sustained a fracture in his arm. The minister immediately rushed to the king's assistance, lifted him tenderly, and bandaging the king's arm with his upper cloth, uttered in his characteristic way, "God, this is also another līlā (sport) of Yours!" The irate king could contain himself no longer. He burst out, "God, God, God! What God! I am sick of hearing your frequent reference to God. Here I am writhing in pain and subject to a paroxysm of sorrow. You, instead of pitying me and coming to my succour, call upon God to witness this event and go about praising Him. I cannot tolerate this any more. Here and now I order you. Harken to what I say. Before you take the name of God in my presence any more, you shall, duty bound, beyond doubt, answer my questions. Here they are."

"Who is God? In which direction is He looking? What can He do? I give you a month's time to give me convincing answers; else you will be beheaded. Stand not in my presence. Till then, goodbye!"

The minister who was taken by surprise at this turn of the tide, was at his wit's end as to what to do. 'Anyone could ask such questions about God, but to give convincing answers about God who is beyond description, only a God should come,' he felt. Yet his faith in God was unshakable. He knew God would not let him down. He remembered the lines from the Gītā, 'My devotee never comes to naught.' Heart within and God overhead, he wended his way through the halls of Brahmasūtras, down the amphitheatres of Upaniṣads, into the chambers of objective sciences, but none of these could give satisfactory answers to those three questions. Tired and spent, sad and dejected, deep in thought, he traced his steps to his abode. Sorrow and worry destroyed his solid calm and content.

Days rolled by. Twenty-eight days had sped by on wings but there was no sign of any forthcoming relief for the anguished soul of the minister. His faith in God was shaken. Weighed down by the thought of certain death, the minister lost all taste for food. The cook of his abode, noticing the change in his master, tried to induce him to eat the savoury and delicious dishes, but in vain. The minister had in these twenty-eight days become lean, lanky and careworn. The cook who loved his master very much and whose devotion to his master was immense, wishing to unburden the weight of sorrow that was obviously troubling the master, said, "Master mine, please pardon me for my impertinence. Though I have no right to question you, my love breaking its bonds, prompts me to ask you why your face is pale and your cheeks wan. What ails you? You have not eaten food for several days. Is anything wrong with my cooking? Is anything wrong with me? Is anything wrong anywhere?

Please tell me. Let me, with the native intelligence God has given me, try to help you out in my humble way."

Touched by the love, sincerity and devotion of the cook, the minister, much as he knew that the solution to the problem was beyond the capacity of the cook, told him, "My problem is too subtle for even the wisest wits. How then can you solve it? Yet, to please your curiosity, I shall unburden myself". So saying, he told the cook all that had happened. He concluded, "My dear, cook, while I appreciate your unbounded love and devotion to me, I will have to pity you, for you will not have any work in my house after two days."

The cook mused for a while and then said, "Beloved master, I have a request to make. This body of mine has been fattened by the substance that I ate while in thy service! Please give me the chance to serve you now at this crucial hour. Permit me, please, to go as your deputy to the king and answer these questions. If I fail, I do not mind being beheaded. Gladly will I lay down my life for you who have gladdened my heart these many summers." Thus urged, the minister who did not know whether to laugh or to weep at this foolhardiness of his cook, said, "I can well understand your devotion for me. But that should not blind me to the fact that these are ticklish questions, beating the ken of even a sapient sage. Hence desist from this foolhardiness". But the cook persisted. "Master mine, even from the slime and the slush a lotus might bloom. What is not possible for God? If God wills, He can play through me and save my master. Hence please allow me to go and answer these questions as your deputy". The minister said, "If that is God's will, you may go. I too, am prepared to meet death with you."

It was the last day of the month. The cook, in tattered attire wended his way to the palace. The king in the meanwhile, was sure that the minister would not turn up with the answers. As he was gloating within himself at the sagacious way in which he had dispensed with the services of the troublesome minister who irritated him by his talk of God, a messenger came in and told him that the minister had sent his cook as a deputy to answer the king's questions. The king thought that this was a joke, yet he ordered the cook to be ushered in. When he was brought in, the king asked the cook whether he was ready to answer his questions. The cook said that he was. The king wanted the cook to be fed well and clothed well first and then brought to the court that evening. Soon messengers were sent to fetch the courtiers.

The court was convened that evening. The ministers in their nicest apparel, the spruce courtiers and the city fathers decked in robes befitting the occasion, gathered there with the gentry of the land. The king was on the throne. The cook

clothed in robes befitting the court, stood before the king with folded arms. Only the minister was not there. All else were present. The king asked the cook whether he was ready to answer the questions. The cook said, "Your Highness, I am prepared to answer your questions on one condition. Ours is a land of ancient culture. It is your Highness's duty to uphold the tradition and culture of our country. It is a tradition in our country to give the teacher an elevated place. The student ought to sit on the floor. Now since you are posing your doubts as questions, you are the student, and since I am the one to give the answers, I take the place of a teacher. So I should sit in an elevated place and you should sit on the floor. If your Majesty is prepared to abide by this tradition throughout the duration of the discussion, I have no objection to answering your questions."

The king frowned. He did not like the turn of events. Yet, this was an assembly where everyone expected him to uphold the tradition of the country and besides, he was pining to know what answers would issue from so plebeian a cook, he conceded the cook's demands. So, with considerable reluctance he said, "So be it. You sit on my throne and I, during the deliberations, will sit on the floor." The cook went and sat on the throne, and the king, on the floor. The cook said, "Now you can pose your questions".

The king said, "Who is God?"

The cook said, "As long as I am seated on the throne you have to obey my commands as if they were coming from a king. Now I want immediately, a black milch cow and a cowherd ready to milch her." The king saw to it that they brought them in. Giving a silver tumbler to the cowherd, the cook-turned-king asked him to milk the cow. Showing the milk to the king, the cook asked, "What is the colour of the milk? How did the white milk come from the black cow?"

The king burst into laughter and said, "Is this a question to ask? Do you not know that it is not the skin of the cow that gives the milk but the food eaten by the cow that is transformed into milk?"

The cook-turned-king immediately ordered that a small quantity of everything that the cow had eaten and drunk during the previous twenty-four hours be brought. In a few minutes, on a silver plate, a small quantity of fodder, green grass, hay, gram, and a tumbler of water were brought. Handing over the plate with its contents to the king, the cook said, "Here is a little of everything the cow ate and drank during the last 24 hours. Can you or anyone else here make milk from these?"

There was complete silence. No one came forward. Addressing the king, the cook said, "Now king, you know very well that neither you nor anyone here can make milk out of these. But there is one person who can do this. He is called God. Please try to know Him."

There was an embarrassed look on the king's face. "What is your next question?" asked the cook-turned-king. With considerably less pride in his voice, the king asked, "In which direction is God looking?"

The cook immediately ordered a candle to be lit; when it was done, he asked the king, "Look at the candle and tell me in which direction the light is turned. In that direction God is looking."

The king was silenced. The colour drained from his face. The court was dumbfounded. Stark silence prevailed for a time. It was broken by a slight commotion at the door. The minister who did not know what was happening in the court, who did not know that the applecart had been upset and that the tables had been turned, came in prepared to receive the death penalty. He walked in with his head down in shame. The audience who saw him enter, were all admiration for him for sending so wise a deputy to answer the questions. In reverence, all gave way for the minister to walk to his seat. Without lifting his head even once, the minister went and occupied his seat. He was startled to hear the voice of his cook who was sitting on the throne and the king on the floor. The cook said to the king, "What is your third question?" The minister's surprise was all the more when he heard the king, with a feeble voice, in a humble way say, "What can God do?"

The cook replied, "You have now seen what God can do to you and me. You the mighty man of the country, the rightful ruler of the kingdom, are now sitting on the floor like a stark plebeian. I, a poor cook, who cannot afford to buy even a nice garment, am now sitting on the august throne, reigning supreme over the noble gathering, commanding all of you and you too, have been obeying my every behest. Your minister, whom you thought you would behead, is sitting there victorious, having answered all your questions through his deputy. That is what God can do to all of us. He can make a small man great and a great man small in no time. He can dry up the oceans or level the mighty mountains by a mere thought of His. All this that thou beholdest are His glory. He can save anyone from death at any time for He is the supreme ruler, controller, governor and benefactor. He is there everywhere. He is subtler than the subtlest, swifter than the swiftest and mightier than the mightiest, yet, He is motionless. He is solid, calm, almighty, eternal and the immutable infinite Self. Befriend Him. Bow down to Him. Surrender to Him. Seek Him and discover Him. Nothing takes place without His will. His will be done."

Getting down from the throne and bowing to the king, the cook added, " Your Highness, please pardon me for making you sit on the floor. Be pleased to occupy your throne. Pardon me please, for the peculiar way in which I answered your questions. That was the only way to save the life of my master whom I love, revere and adore".

A mighty transformation had come over the king. Gone was his pride. Spent was his vanity. True to the line of descent from which he came, he saw the hand of God in everything. Turning to the dazed minister, he said, " I am sorry I gave you a lot of trouble and anxiety. Your cook has opened my eyes to the mysteries of God. Let us all bow to His wishes."

Is it not likewise that many of us, drunk with the wine of power, position, status, wealth and possession, go about strutting and cackling, 'That enemy has been slain by me, and the other also I will destroy. I am the Lord, I am the enjoyer, I am perfect, powerful and happy. Who else is equal to me? I will sacrifice people and distribute favours as I like. All should bow down to me.' And do we not see the wheel of fortune turn a full circle and crush under its inexorable wheel the might and main of the vain and the wicked, the malicious and the malevolent? But when even such a wicked one were to be, even by chance, in the just company of a pious soul like the minister, salvation is certain, Knowledge dawns and the cloud of ignorance is dispelled. Even from the meanest creature that blooms, the most chaste wisdom can come to solve the subtlest problem that can trouble even the wisest sage. This parable enlightens us with the truth that God is omnipotent, omnipresent and omniscient. His will be done. Ours is simply to surrender to Him and carry out His behests.

3. The Unseen Hand of God

It was altogether an old world place. Life was ambling in a leisurely fashion. The hurry, the hectic activity and the devilish dance of the greed for lucre had not stuck roots into the unsophisticated minds of the innocent dwellers of this sacred land of Bhārata. Trades were many, crafts were varied and each and every man stuck to his trade, profession or craft with a zest for work, and so, life was pleasant. The length and breadth of Bhārata was spanned by numerous hamlets serving as the backbone of Bhārata. From one such hamlet, a young rustic, with chiselled features, guileless mien, strong and sturdy limbs, and with a healthy outlook on life, made his way towards the town of Tirupati, the abode of the Lord of the seven hills. In this sacred town lived a Mahanta, a man of importance, noted for his generosity of spirit, nobleness of heart and subtlety of intellect.

This Mahanta, himself a mighty owner of an estate, had taken on his shoulders the responsibility of manning a Trust of a vast property which included temples, houses, big establishments, forests and lands both wet and dry. To this man did the rustic wend his way. When this rustic went to his dwelling, he heard that the Mahanta had just gone and so, with quickened pace he hurried forward to have a tryst with him. Soon he espied him near the lush green fields skirting the town. Paying his obeisance to the Mahanta he said, "Mahārāja, I hail from a neighbouring hamlet. I am in search of work. I am prepared to take up any kind of work that your honour is pleased to give. Please help me." The Mahanta noticed that the youth was bright in appearance, strong of limbs, simple in habits, obedient in nature and of an honest disposition. He said, "Well lad, I do feel like helping you. But, at present there is no job vacant in my estate. So I do not know how I can help you". The rustic, not to be so easily outwitted, said, "Mahārāja, even if no job is vacant, if your honour should deign to help me, I would be blessed. If your honour is pleased, you could allot me a piece of land. It matters little where it is or how it is. I am strong of limb, of a persevering kind and of an unbending will. I can work hard. I deter not from drudgery". The Mahanta was in a good mood and so, he felt that he should help him at any cost. His eyes fell just then on the northern part of the rugged road on which they were standing. It was dry land, utterly rugged in nature and unfit for cultivation. But that was the only part not allotted, and so, pointing out that piece of land to the rustic he said, "Lad, look here, this is the only piece that has not been allotted. I do not know whether this will be of any use to you. If you wish, you can occupy it and put it to use." The youth, on hearing this, was beside himself with joy; and so said, "A thousand thanks to your honour. I do not know how I should express my joy and gratitude. May your tribe increase"! The Mahanta moved on.

The youth now inspected the piece of land. No doubt it was a dry land, uncultivable. Yet, where there is a will there is a way. He set himself to work. Borrowing a crowbar, a spade and a billhook he soon cleared the land of all the shrubs. Now he started loosening the soil. But very severe was the task, for the land was punctuated here and there with rocks, some very huge. But the lad was up to the task. He was of a plodding type and so, he was able to remove all of them within a week. He began to loosen the soil. When he reached a depth of three feet, he found that the soil was virgin, red in colour. Now, borrowing a hammer and a crowbar from the neighbourhood, he broke the huge rocks he had hauled out of the field. He thought of putting even these

rocks to use. Soon he arranged them around the field, thus building a fence for the field. The next day he approached a kindly farmer and requested him to spare for his use, his bullocks and the plough just for two days. He promised the farmer that in return for this kind act, he would help him with his farming for four days. The farmer agreed and felt that it was a just deal, and so spared for the rustic, the bullocks and the plough. The rustic first fulfilled his promise and then began to plough his land. Soon he dug a well in one corner of his land and drawing the water from the well, irrigated his field. Day in and day out, he laboured in his field.

Six months passed. The sky smiled, the rains blessed the earth at the right season and everything went well with the cultivation without a let or hindrance. The harvest season came. Nature blessed the rustic with a bountiful and bumper crop. The youth in all earnestness began harvesting the crops. As he was harvesting, he saw the Mahanta with his retinue of attendants passing that way. At the sight of the Mahanta, the rustic's heart welled up with thoughtful gratitude. So, in all devotion, he ran thither and falling at his feet said, "Mahārāja, I am ever indebted to you for all that you have done for me. Whenever I think of you, my cheeks are bedewed with tears of thoughtful gratitude. I do not know how I should repay you for your benevolence". The Mahanta was bewildered to see a stranger falling at his feet and expressing words of gratitude. So he said, "O, youth, who are you and what have I done for you and why should you thank me?" In the routine of the Mahanta, allotment of land to imploring peasants was done so often that he could scarcely recall when he had given this lad the right over the land. But those in his retinue remembered it. The youth now said, "Mahārāja, look this way. See how glorious your fields are! Just see what a bountiful and golden harvest is going on there! It is all thine and due to thy grace. Had not your honour allotted this piece of land to me, I could not have raised those crops. I am ever indebted to thee, master". The Mahanta now turned towards that side and seeing the bountiful harvest said, "Is this my land? Did I allot it to you? Let me refresh my memory. Well, was not this a rugged piece of dry land unfit for cultivation? How is it you have transformed it into a lush golden field brimming with a beautiful harvest? All this beats my understanding. The youth said, "Master, it is all thy grace. It was thy land. Six months back you allotted it to me. I worked on it zealously and so, the land smiled and blessed us. It is all thine, my master".

The kindly Mahanta said, "Praise the Lord, O youth! I have not done anything. I gave you only a poor allotment of a rugged piece of uncultivable land. God willed that your husbandry should be rewarded and He willed that this rugged piece of land should smile, and so have you been successful. Hence, offer your thanks unto God. I do not deserve your thanks". The youth, who till then had not thought of God, said, "Mahārāja, excuse me for my impertinence. I know of no God. This much I know well. You allotted me this piece. I worked day in and day out and, with my unbending will, ploughed laboriously, cultivated cautiously, tended carefully and irrigated industriously and so, here we have this bountiful harvest. What has God done to deserve my thanks?" The Mahanta said, "Lad, you are ignorant. I clearly see the hand of God in every act of yours. This piece of rugged land was there even before you came here. It was God who brought you here. It was He who timed your tryst with me; for you saw me when I was standing very near this plot. So my allotting this piece of land to you is God's Will. It was He who gave me a charitable disposition at that time or else I would not have given you this land. It was He who brought you and the land together. It was He who blessed you with the strength of limb, an unbending will, perseverance and tenacity of purpose. It was He who sent the rains in the right season. It was He who planted in the heart of the neighbouring farmer the kindness which made him help you with the bullocks and the plough. So it is all God's work. So praise God". The youth was still unconvinced. He said, "Mahārāja, excuse me. This little head of mine cannot understand all this that you say about God. One thing alone I understand and that is, you are my sole benefactor. I revere you and prostrate to you". The Mahanta smiled, and lifting his hands to the heavens said, "Lord, mysterious are Thy ways. I see Thy hand in every act that goes on here." So saying he moved on.

This parable exemplifies stanza 16, Chapter 13 of the *Bhagavad-gītā*, which says, 'He is without and within all beings. He is unmoving and also moving. He is too subtle to be known. He is far away, yet is He near'.

God is the subtlest of the subtle. So to realise Him subtlety is needed. When a poet writes a poem, it is not only the fingers that write but the contemplative mind behind the fingers that prod them to write. So, to understand the poem, the reader has to develop the subtlety to lift himself to the level of the poet. So too, to understand and realise God who is the warp and weft of creation, the seeker should develop subtlety. 'Sūkṣmatvattad avijñeyaṁ'. Here in this parable, the Mahanta had the subtlety to understand the hand of God in all that had happened, whereas the rustic had not developed that subtlety though he was hardworking, persevering and painstaking.

4. The King of Kāśī

In the days of old, in the city of Kāśī, its people followed a peculiar political philosophy, according to which anyone of its citizens could become its ruler just for the asking. The tenure of rulership was five years. But, after the fifth year, the king would be bound hand and foot, ferried across the river Ganga to the other bank and thrown as a prey to the wild and hungry beasts infesting the forest on the other side of the river. So, very few chose to become the king. The few that did choose were those that felt that at least for a brief period of five years they could live in regal splendour and be above want. When the term of rulership came to a close, many a king wished he had not chosen the self ordained doom, for mercilessly and speedily was he despatched by the ministers to the other bank of the river to face his doom. Not a single king had escaped this doom. So, prudent people judiciously avoided this crown of thorns.

It was the custom of the people to gather on the bank of the river Ganga every fifth year to see the king making his unceremonious exit. On such occasions, they invariably heard the piteous entreaties of the king for a lease of life which, as was usual, fell on deaf ears. But on one such occasion, they were surprised to see a king coming to the wharf maintaining his regal dignity, with a silent composure of serenity. The king was followed by his retinue of ministers. The boat was there ready for the king to embark.

Looking at the ministers, the king said, "Well, am I not your king until I reach the other bank of the river?" They in unison said, "Yes, your Majesty". The king said, "In that case I feel I have not been honoured properly. This boat is not rigged properly. It is unbecoming of a king to sit on the hard plank of the boat. So get me cushions and pillows and arrange them in such a way that I can have a comfortable trip to the other bank of the Ganga." The ministers carried out the king's command immediately. The king's seat was made comfortable. The king smiled at them and in a cheerful way took leave of them.

The old ferryman who took charge of the king, was surprised to see the king in good cheer. He thought that the king was perhaps unaware of his doom. Ferrying the boat slowly, eyeing the king askance, he asked the king how he could keep himself cool and collected in spite of the fact that soon he would meet his doom. On hearing this, the king laughed loudly and burst into a song of joy. The ferryman was even more perplexed. He mused for a while and said to the king, "If Your Majesty is thinking of escaping from me, I have to say humbly but firmly that I, at all costs, will avert such a contingency. I have to take all precautions. So permit me, Your Majesty, to bind you to your seat". The king again laughed, but permitted himself to be bound to the seat.

The boat had sailed half way when the ferryman asked the king whether he was not afraid of the wild beasts on the other bank of the river. The king, in surprise, uttered, "What did you say? Wild beasts! Where? On the other side of the Ganga? Oh! then, innocent man, you do not know what has happened. I shall tell you what I did. Listen for a while. This shows that you have not been to the other bank of the river for the past five years, nor have you noticed the trafficking that has been going on all these five years on the waters of this mighty river. There is no wild forest on the other side of this river, and there are no wild beasts either. I was not like the other kings when I was ruling the country. Right from the moment I assumed kingship, the thought that I would be unceremoniously and mercilessly despatched to my doom after my tenure of rulership, haunted me. I felt I should find a way out. Though at first, this haunting thought of my doom rankled me and could have prevented me from enjoying the comforts of kingship, I mastered myself and mustering the

powers of my sagacious mind, with a gusto, began to enjoy the comforts. I drew up a five year plan. I could, of course, not avert going to the other bank of the Ganga after the fifth year. But I felt I had the power in me to make a heaven out of hell. So I decided to make the forest on the other bank of the Ganga, which till now was a hell to all the other rulers, a heaven for me. So, during the first year of my rule, I sent a platoon of hunters and ordered them to destroy all the wild animals in the forest on the other bank of the river. In the second year, I sent two thousand woodcutters to fell the trees and clear the forest. In the third year, I sent worker masons, architects and engineers there and made them build lovely palaces, develop pleasure gardens, beautiful parks, exquisite pleasure bowers, handsome swimming pools and lovely stadia for me and thus I made it a paradise of pleasures. In the fourth year, I selected trustworthy and loyal men from my court, appointed them as ministers, bade them go thither and plan how the country could be made beautiful, ruled righteously and well. In the fifth year, picking and choosing people who are good, virtuous and loyal to me, I ordered them to migrate to Vyāsa Kāśī – for that is the name I have given the new city, conferring on them the ownership of houses they now occupy. Now I am bound for that place to assume kingship of that city. Oh! ferryman, look for yourself how grand my city is, for we are nearing it now. Just glance that way. Do not you see my ministers in their best, with garlands in their hands, ready to welcome me? Do you not see the musicians, pipers and symphonists with their musical appurtenances rendering a soulful song of ecstasy welcoming me, their cherished Lord? There will I rule permanently, unhampered by any of your pentagonal pestilences. I have mastered my fate. Am I not a man of destiny? If you want, you too can come and be my ferryman."

The ferryman did see on the other bank of the river the mighty city of splendour and glory. He saw also the colourful gathering awaiting their king. A caparisoned elephant waited with its howdah, ready to receive the king! Thither did the king alight. In mute wonder did the ferryman gaze on and on at the glorious spectacle. From then on, the king spent his days in gay abandon, living his full span of life, ruling righteously and augustly the land of Vyāsa Kāśī.

The life that we lead in this world is this Kāśī. We are the self-appointed rulers of our lives. But there is a tenure for our stay here. Not a second more than the time allotted to us, will we be allowed to live here. We lay waste our precious powers, thoughtlessly vegetating, earning, spending, breeding and indulging in frivolous pleasures. Then, when the sad end comes, we blame our fate, our stars, nay even our Gods, not realising that it is all of our own making. Instead, if we too, like the king of Vyāsa Kāśī can, with foresight and farsightedness, strive on with determination, discrimination and steadfastness. We can chalk out for ourselves a charter of happiness and a glorious era of eternal peace and unalloyed bliss. At the same time, we can face the challenges of the interaction of the forces in a world limited by space, time and causation.

This inherent power in us to overcome our fate is in Sanskrit called puruṣārtha. Fate is undoubtedly the result of our past actions. By using this inherent power in us, we can lift ourselves to such heights where the effect of the forces of fate will not be felt by us. This, in short, is what the parable tells us.

5. Even This Will Pass Away

There was no one in the business world in India who did not know Krishnacharan. He was the multimillionaire who had established a regular supply of manufactured goods from India to the foreign countries, thereby earning for India the much needed foreign exchange. Krishnacharan had risen from the lowest level of society to the highest by his tenacity of purpose, nobility of thought, indefatigable industry and fearless spirit. He was a devotee of Lord Kṛṣṇa. The branches of his business spanned the length and breadth of India. People at home and abroad liked him for his simplicity, frankness and firmness. For a long time he had no children. He prayed to God day and night to bless him with a child. He went on a pilgrimage to many holy places in India. Days passed. He had reached his 40th year. It was then that God blessed him with a son.

Krishnacharan paid special attention to the upbringing of the child. He wanted his son, Mrityunjaya, for that was the name he had given him, to become a dynamic technocrat. The child too, showed signs of the spirit of a technocrat in him. The child looked curiously and eagerly at all the automatic toys placed in his hands. He began tinkering with them. As time went on, Mrityunjaya left the nurse's arms to go to school. He distinguished himself at school by standing first in the class. The teachers marvelled at the uncommon genius displayed by the tiny boy. He was good not only inside the classroom but also outside. He distinguished himself in sports and games too. Soon he left the school to join the University.

Krishnacharan paid attention to the boy and so the boy was not spoilt. Mrityunjaya had developed in him powers of perception so keenly that he was able to remember and reproduce whatever he had seen or heard only once. Blessed with a unique power of memory and endowed with the dexterity of hands, he did well at college and soon joined an Institute of Technology. There too, he was head and shoulders above his classmates. Finishing his course, he came out of the Institute standing first in the order of merit.

Now Krishnacharan was sixty one. His body had begun to show signs of ageing and he felt a lassitude of spirit. He felt he should withdraw from the hectic business and devote more of his time to spiritual activities. So he wanted his son Mrityunjaya to relieve him of the burden of running the business, which he had spread in a network throughout the length and breadth of India. One day he called his son and expressed to him his desire. Mrutyunjaya loved his father deeply, but was not prepared for this. He, with all respect for his father, told him that he was still young and inexperienced and hence would not be able to take up on his shoulders the management of the business and run it as efficiently as his father had done. Further, he said that his ambition was to get a Doctorate degree in Technology. He told his father that if he was permitted, he would like to go to U.S.A., work for his doctorate, learn the secrets of business there and return with added knowledge. Then he would willingly lift the load off his father's shoulders. The father, who was patiently listening to him all the while, saw that there was a point in this and so conceded to his son's request.

Mrityunjaya had already corresponded with the universities in U.S.A., and in one of them he had already got a seat as a research student. Now he got busy, getting his passport and visa. The day of his departure, too, was fixed. It was a Friday. He came to his father's room to take leave of him. When Krishnacharan looked at his son, his love for him overpowered him for a brief spell, and his eyes were bedewed with tears of love. The thought of separation was troubling him. Soon, manning his emotions, Krishnacharan took from out of his chest of drawers a diamond ring he had made for his son. Giving it to him he said, "Mrityunjaya, here is a gift. May this be the Lord of your emotions. I give this to you now. May this gift give you strength of limb and power of mind to weather the storms of life; this is my prayer today. I know you dislike wearing rings. Yet, because of your love for me, wear this. Should you, at any time in the future, feel disheartened and disappointed (God forbid such a contingency), go to a quiet corner, sit comfortably, remove the ring from your finger and play with it, tossing it in the air and catching it again for a while. That is all my parting advice to you. May the household Gods I worship day in and day out, protect you. Godspeed to you". Mrityunjaya did not then understand why his father was tendering such a queer piece of advice. Yet, out of love and respect for him, he did not question him. Paying obeisance to his father he took leave of him.

Mrityunjaya reached U.S.A. and plunged himself in the research work with heart and soul. During the short spell of vacation, he visited, by appointment, various industries around the place and learnt the knowhow of all. Two years passed and he got his doctorate degree. By then he had cultivated a friendship of some of the wealthy people there. Seeing in this young man signs of success, the wealthy people there requested him to stay there and start an industry, the finance for which they would bear. The enthusiastic Mrityunjaya, finding a field opening out for him, wrote to his father and obtained his consent. 'Where there is a will there is a way.' Mrityunjaya's will was firm and his way began to flourish. Soon he had made giant strides in the industrial field and the instruments he manufactured, captured the market in a sweep. He had established a name for himself in the technical world. His assets soon increased. He too became not only a working partner but also a financing one. For three years his business flourished. At the beginning of the fourth year there was a trade depression and there was a sudden fall in the market rates of the goods he had stocked. There was an unprecedented heavy loss in his business. He was shocked. He had not anticipated this. Many wealthy partners began pressing him to return their capital. How could he face them now? All the capital he had, he had invested in the industry. He was now desperate, disappointed and dumbfounded. He felt his career had come to a miserable end. What would his father, who had never known failure, think of him, if he heard of his son's failure?

Mrityunjaya was in a fix. Should he or should he not write to his father about his loss? No doubt, his father could lift him from the morass, but it would mean that he was inefficient in business. The conflict within was so great that in a desperate mood, he thought of committing suicide. Late that night he drove towards a bridge spanning a mighty river. The road was deserted. Mrityunjaya was desperate. He got down from the car, walked towards the railings, stood towards the railings, ready to plunge longhead into the river. For a while he began to reminisce. A train of thoughts passed through his mind. He thought of his father and remembered his parting advice. He then looked at the ring his father had given him. He felt he should, before ending his life, satisfy the queer wish of his father.

Turning round, he jumped back onto the pavement. He found no one there. A street lamp was illumining the emptiness of the place. Mrityunjaya spread his kerchief on the pavement and sat on it. Removing the ring he began playing with it. As he was tossing it, his eyes caught sight of an inscription engraved on the inner side of the ring. His heart missed a beat! He had hitherto never cared to look at the inner side of the ring. Now, inspite of himself, he was curiously looking at the inscription. He read it word by word. Lo! it said, 'EVEN THIS WILL PASS AWAY'. He pondered for a while. Was his father, now miles and miles away, giving him, in troubled waters, a message? Will even this trade depression pass away? Is it merely just a passing phase?

He felt as if his father was near him in flesh and blood, asking him not to commit the rash act. Perhaps his father had

meaningfully named him Mrityunjaya and so he must now win over death. He felt his previous resolve slowly losing its hold on him. He got up, jumped into his car, went back to his house and thought deeply for a while. He had established a name as an honest businessman. Various financing corporations there knew of his honesty, integrity and ability. Many a time they had offered to finance his endeavours, but he somehow had declined. Why should he not make use of their offer now? Especially there was one corporation working round the clock. He rang them up and asked if the offer still stood. He was glad to hear from the corporators that they considered it their fortune to finance him. He requested them to credit to his account a certain amount, and they did. The next morning he rang his partners and asked them to come and collect their share capital, if they so desired. They were all surprised! 'How could Mrityunjaya, who was broken the previous night, have overnight got ready to disburse them their capital'?, they thought. They deliberated among themselves and came to the conclusion that they should continue as partners. Mrityunjaya felt elated. Again, with redoubled energy he plunged into business. At the end of the year he found himself in clover again. The business prospered. Mrityunjaya constantly reminded himself of the message in the ring, 'Even this will pass away'. From then on he felt a spirit of equanimity deliberating his actions. He was neither elated by success nor depressed by failure. He took everything in his stride and dealt with it in an equanimous way. Acquiring a lot of fortune, he returned to his father and gave him at last the rest he was yearning for.

6. The Genie and The Brahmin

In a quiet sequestered valley south of the Vindhya mountains, there lived an unsophisticated brood of guileless peasants in amity, friendship and cooperation. For them summer smiled, winter winced, spring danced and autumn showered its plenty. Their days were spent judiciously in harmonious work, play and prayer. But time sports and brings in its wake its store of sorrows. A severe famine rocked the valley, blighting its flora and fauna and scourging its simple peasants of artless kind. So severe was the famine that the peasants forgot all their good ways of living and began quarrelling among themselves, for the crumbs that still remained to satisfy their ravenous hunger.

There lived amidst these peasants a thin, emaciated, decrepit old brahmin, burdened with a large family. This old man, though not graced with nature's plenty, was blessed with fourteen children. Alas! pinched with poverty, living in titanic glooms and fear of abject penury, with a nagging wife, pestering children and teasing neighbours, he did not know how to ward off the mounting trouble. The hut in which he lived was a thatched one. Its roof was in shambles, letting in the scorching rays in summer and the biting cold of the chaffing wind in winter. Though he was weak in body, he had an unbending will and so he did not desert his family. Any work he was prepared to do, but how could work be procured in a blighted land scourged with famine? So he was at his wit's end.

Weighed down by sorrows, doubly bent by despair and age, the brahmin stood under a red rock, holding in his hands a handful of dust symbolic of the fear of extermination. Even in that mood of despair, there flitted lightly through his troubled mind a hymn from the Vedas. It lightened his heart. For a moment he caught a glimpse of that peace that passeth all understanding. Soon flashed past his mind a sapient thought. He asked himself, "Why do I not seek the sage in the yonder forest and bathe in the peace of his benign presence?" The thought manifested itself as action and soon he repaired to the forest.

It was evening time. The parched earth pocked with a thousand gaping mouths presented a pitiful sight. Dust danced everywhere. The sweltering wind carried with it his smouldering heart. The tired brahmin, with a wearied spirit, reached the hermitage of the sage. The peace of the place assuaged his tormented soul. He sat for a while on the ledge, giving his aching limbs a short repose. The sage was in samādhi. The brahmin waited outside unwilling to disturb the sage in samādhi. After a while the sage, opening his eyes, espied the brahmin with the unkempt beard and haggard looks. He asked him to come in. Then he beckoned him to be seated on the mat. Refreshing the brahmin with a glass of cool water, he enquired after his welfare. The sage had not stirred out of his retreat for more than three months, and so, he did not know that the people of the valley were in dire straits. The brahmin apprised him of the situation. He begged the sage to help him out of the crisis through which he was passing. The sage smiled lovingly and said, "May peace and plenty be there for the children of immortality. Worry not, blessed soul, the Lord knows how to relieve you of your burden. Trust in Him and surrender to Him. He will not desert you. Now go out, take a dip in the yonder pond and then come here. I have a tryst with you. It is a tryst of destiny for you and your fellowmen!" The brahmin hastened to the pond, had a holy dip, said his evening prayers and returned to the sage. The sage had, in the meanwhile lighted a jyoti with its five sparkling wicks. Outside, the birds that had come to roost were chirping and cawing and slowly settling down. The entire place was permeated with the peace of a just soul – the sapient sage was a soul of peace with whom nature was at peace.

The sage sat opposite the brahmin and bade him repeat with him a sacred mantra, word symbol representing and expressing a particular view of God and the universe it stands for. Initiating him into its secret import he said, "This sacred mantra that I have given you now is the Lord of a powerful genie. If you chant this mantra with faith and devotion, a powerful genie will appear before you to act according to your behests. You can make use of this genie and overcome all your troubles and bring untold blessings to your fellowmen too. Now go forth into your hamlet with a will to serve humankind sincerely and selflessly. But mind you, there is a string attached to this mantra. When once you invoke the genie, you will have to keep him constantly engaged, else, he will eat you up. Bear this in mind, may the Gods give you peace and plenty and may your service be fruitful". The brahmin felt himself thrice blessed. The mantra with which he had been initiated gave him a compelling grace, an enchanting beauty, a pleasant aura and a self-evident glow of holiness. He thought he could easily keep the genie ever engaged. He offered his obeisance to the sage, and taking leave of him, happily came back to his hut.

His wife and children, who had missed him for more than two hours, were eagerly awaiting his arrival. The brahmin bade his wife and children go out for a while, promising them a sumptuous dinner soon. Then retiring to a corner of his hut, he invoked the genie. There appeared before

him the genie in all his hideousness! Bowing low before the brahmin he said, "Master, what do you want of me? Order and it shall be accomplished!" The brahmin, beside himself with joy, ordered the genie to serve them a sumptuous dinner. In a trice of time, the genie placed before them all golden bowls and silver plates laden with savoury dishes of several kinds. The brahmin, calling in his kids and wife, shared with them the rich repast. Now he ordered the genie to convert the hut into a lovely palace. The genie immediately changed the hut into a lovely palace. The brahmin ordered him to equip the palace with beautiful furniture and a rich store of all things needed for him and his family. This, too, the genie did in a fraction of a second. Now the genie wanted him to give him some more work. The brahmin, in a moment of expansion, thought of the people of the valley; and so, asked the genie to bring cheer and comfort to the teeming hundreds in the hamlets. The genie soon changed the hamlets into a heaven of bliss. The people of the valley were beside themselves with joy at this unexpected turn of events. Now the genie was urging the brahmin to give him some more work. The brahmin, full to the brim physically, mentally completely satisfied, intellectually at ease with his own self, did not know what more to order. The genie was pestering him for work. The brahmin was at his wit's end. He stood there like a statue, unable to think of anything. The genie, finding that work was not forthcoming, rushed at the brahmin to eat him up. The frightened brahmin, sensing the danger, rushed out of the house screaming for help. He was hotly pursued by the powerful genie. The people of the valley felt themselves powerless before the all-powerful genie.

The brahmin took to his heels, running this way and that. But with an unperturbed pace, unhurrying chase and with deliberate speed, the strong feet of the genie followed the brahmin wherever he went. Across the edge of the valley, fled the brahmin seeking shelter behind bars of the secure houses of his fellowmen from pillar to post. But help was not forthcoming. The genie was gaining ground. Now the brahmin thought of the sage, and so, he rushed to the forest. Fear gave him wings and in a trice of time he was at the hermitage. Prostrating to the sage he cried for shelter. The aged sage said, "Brother mine, what more dost thou need? Why this fretting and fuming, this sweating and simmering? Speak out your thoughts. God will help you". The desperate brahmin said, "Gurumahārāja, it is the genie! The genie is chasing me to eat me up. I know not how to keep him ever engaged. Please take away the genie. I want nothing". The sage smiled and said, "Did I not tell you that you should keep him ever engaged? Now even I cannot take away the genie. But I can tender you advice which, if you follow, you can keep the genie under your service and at the same time keep him ever engaged". Aghast with wonder, the brahmin said, "Master mine, please tell me what it is and I shall follow it implicitly". The Master then said, "Go home now and fix a long pole in the centre of your courtyard. Then order the genie to go up and down the pole until you ask him to stop. Whenever you are in need of his service, call him back from the pole and when there is no work, make him go up and down the pole continuously. The brahmin bowed to the sage and running to the palace, called the genie and ordered him to fix a long pole in the centre of the courtyard and then told him to go up and down the pole until he wanted him to stop. The genie was thus brought under control and the brahmin from that moment felt happy, for he had the service of the genie and at the same time, he was able to keep him ever engaged.

Our mind is the genie. It must always be engaged, for mind is thought flow. When thoughts end, the mind ceases to be a mind. This is the mind that we have invoked to fulfil our desires in this grand pilgrimage from the womb to the tomb. But this mind should be continually on the march. An idle mind is a devil's workshop. The mind that is the genie, will devour you if you do not keep it constantly engaged. So the sages tell us that we should make use of the mind in serving us in our day-to-day activities, but when it is not engaged, we ought to plant in it a thought of the Lord of our heart and make the mind dwell on that thought continually, to the exclusion of all other thoughts. This will help us in not only controlling the mind (the genie) but also conserving and preserving our energy by not allowing it to get depleted in the regrets of the past or the anxieties for the future or the excitements in the present.

7. Madhu and The Mathematics Professor

It was the season of examinations. Boys and girls were burning the midnight oil, poring over the leaves of their books. Deep analysis, memorising, subtle reflection and thorough reproduction were the several methods adopted by students during this season. The have-nots in knowledge clustered round the haves in knowledge, like honey bees to blossoms. The haves sharpened their wits recalling, retelling, recapturing and extensively explaining to the have-nots what they had mastered. To the larger community of the happy-go-lucky type of have-nots in knowledge belonged our Madhu. Madhu he was, with no 'Madhu' for reasoning in his physical or metaphysical anatomy. Inasmuch as Mathematics is the whetstone for the wits, Madhu's father, who was a flourishing politician and crossed floors freely, wanted his son to sharpen his wits. Though he had succeeded in politics with his native cunning, he felt that in times to come, one would need a sharper cunning, a subtler sense of wit to gauge the minds of those much muddled ones who pull the strings of political hierarchy. He wanted his son to come up to his expectations of stupendous success in this political gimmicks. Hence, knocking on the back doors of educational institutions, overpowering and overawing the elite who man the institutions, with his overbearing political tinkering, he made way for his son to gain a seat in the undergraduate course in Mathematics. Whether his son deserved the seat or not and whether his son had the taste for it or not, were matters of no importance to him. As a politician, he had many a time fought for the redemption of the underdogs. He considered that he himself and his brethren, the underdogs, needed the patronage, support and financial backing from the Government. To this end he spared no pains. So, having admitted his son Madhu, the apple of his eye, to the Mathematics course, he made him go through the ordeal of differentiation and integration in Calculus, binomial theorem and quadratic equations of all kinds in Algebra. The son, too, plodded through with one step inside the classroom and the other in posh theatres. What kind of performance could one expect from such a student as Madhu, in a field such as Mathematics in which the ruling passion was reason and logic, the twin wings of intellection? Had these been birds, he could have caught them and trapped them. Had they been a commodity, his father would have procured them by his overawing power. But Mathematics treats all the same way, whether they are low brows or high brows. It always says, 'Have you the wit, the sagacity, the tenacity and the perseverance of a genius, then you shall enter. Otherwise, au revoir!' Blessed with none of these, Madhu was trying his very best, hoping against hope, to tide over the crisis of the coming university examinations. His father sensed the son's predicament. Greasing the palm of itching legions that serve the machinery of management of the Board of examination he procured the much hunted for question paper, well in advance.

Armed with this question paper, Madhu, though feeling secure, still felt out of sorts. Just as delicious sweets rarely please a person suffering from diabetes, how could the Mathematics question paper help a student utterly devoid of any mathematical sense? Madhu's mind began to work. He could meet his classmates, rich in mathematical lore and wheedle out the answers from them, but this would let the cat out of the bag, and a re-examination would then loom large. What other way could there be of solving this problem for Madhu? Yes, there was a silver lining to the sable coloured cloud of doubts in him. His Mathematics professor always had a soft corner for him. The professor had taken it as a challenge to inject at least some mathematical sense into his mind which had neither windows nor doors to allow even a ray of mathematical sense! Surely his Mathematics professor would be able to help him out. But he could not tell the professor that he had with him the question paper. So he copied down the questions, each on a separate sheet of paper, and posing them as doubts to be cleared, to the professor's house he wended his way.

Raghava Shastri, the famous professor of Mathematics, had an intuitive brain that could, with razor sharp precision hit at right solutions in the space of a fraction of a second. He needed no books. His brain was fertile, his memory remarkable and the gift of logic gigantic in his mental anatomy. The day Madhu decided to go to this professor's house, there was great unrest in his house. He was on casual leave that day, spending a greater part of his time attending to household chores. When Madhu went in, the professor was walking to and fro in the verandah, as if to assess the dimensions of the floor that touched sprawling feet. Standing near the verandah and looking up at him, Madhu addressed the professor, "Good evening, Sir". The professor turning round, eyeing Madhu as he would a worm, said "Who are you, and what do you want at this hour?" This unnerved Madhu. The professor knew him well. How come then he did not recognise him now? The sheaves of papers in his hand began to flutter in the gentle breeze that was blowing there. Gathering his courage, raising his voice a little, Madhu said, "It is I Sir, Madhu, your student, Sir. I have some doubts in Mathematics Sir". Uttering these words, he offered the papers with the problems to the professor. Without even looking at the papers, the professor, now angry, bawled out, "Mathematics or coothematics, I know nothing about it. I do not know you. Get out of this place". Blood drained from Madhu's face. He became death-pale. Any further conversation he knew, would serve as gasoline to a conflagration of ire of the teacher. So he beat a hasty retreat. When he reached the outer courtyard of the house, unwilling to be so easily defeated in his attempt and not knowing how his professor failed to recognise him, he stood there under a tree, a monument of amazement.

Just then a car purred in the silence at the gate. A boy carrying a leather box emerged from the car and hastily walked towards the house. Then a cute apparition, in a shapely white attire, tip-toed on high heels elegantly towards the portico of the house. Even as Madhu was eyeing all this with curiosity, a young man, spick and span in attire wearing a loose white coat, with his fingers playing on a long black tube with shining metallic ends, followed majestically the elegant apparition in spotless white. Madhu's attention was arrested by this procession. He forgot his problems, forgot his disappointment and began to watch what was going on in his professor's house. The three that came out of the car disappeared into the house. Madhu waited to know the end of this game that was going on inside the house. A full fifteen minutes passed. The young man in loose white coat came out, smiled at the professor and, shaking hands with him, congratulated him. The professor too, who till then was serious, found the muscles of his face relaxing. He too beamed a smile. The young man came down the steps and moved towards his car. The elegant apparition, with the boy by her side also got into the car. Raising a cloud of dust, the car sped away.

Madhu was still standing under the tree. The sun was setting behind the western horizon. In the dull light, he stood there like a statue. Suddenly he was awakened from his reverie by the thunderous voice of the professor, "Who is there standing under the tree?" Madhu's feet moved mechanically towards the professor. Madhu's vocal chords had been benumbed by the torpor of fear in him. He stood near the professor like a symbol of obedience. The professor holding his cupped palm above his eyes, looking at Madhu, suddenly said, "Is it you, Madhu? What brings you here?" Madhu's mind was irresolute like that of Hamlet. 'To speak or not to speak, that's the question. Whether it is nobler to suffer the stings of outrageous ignorance or by opposing, end them'. Madhu overcame the Hamlet in him. He said, "Sir, I have some doubts in Mathematics. Here are the doubts. I do not know how to solve them." The professor said, "Doubts! Oh! Give them to me". Taking the sheaves of papers and going through them, he smiled at Madhu and said, "You do not know even these? Does not matter. Now come, sit here and take down the steps". Madhu eagerly obeyed, and in half an hour he had the solution to all the problems. Success was surely round the corner for him. The professor then asked him, "Any more doubts?" What now bewildered Madhu was why his professor had failed to recognise him some time back and why the professor, so devoted to Mathematics, denied even a nodding acquaintance with Mathematics. So he gave expression to his bewilderment and said, "An hour back when I came here and begged you to clear my doubts, you failed to recognise me and said you knew neither Mathematics nor coothematics. I am yet puzzled how such a thing could happen". The professor burst into laughter and said, "On that! You will not know it now! After you get married, you will certainly understand the predicament in which I was placed. So now, good luck to you. Fare well in the examination and then come and tell me all about your performance". Wondering what these words meant and what his marriage had to do with them, Madhu, with mixed feelings of joy and bewilderment, went out of the house. How could he know the restlessness of a husband whose wife was going through the agony of birth pangs?

Even a man who is very clever, exceedingly capable of seeing the subtle meaning of things and endowed with great intelligence and genius, is sometimes overpowered by the influence of tamas. He then becomes incapable of understanding Reality, though it is clearly present before him in a concrete form. Not only does he not understand the truth, but he also insists that what has been (falsely) projected by him, alone is real. The tāmasika aspect of māyā has such a mighty power.

The agitations caused in the professor's mind by the birth pangs of his beloved wife, produced a veil in his mind which made him die temporarily all Mathematics and the world of Mathematics he was a lord of!

8. The Exhibition

Jayadeva was the ruling monarch of the Sun dynasty. Under his stewardship, the country of Svarṇabhūmi made giant strides in the field of arts, literature, music, commerce and philosophy. His fame spread beyond the seas and the prosperity of the country invited many a foreigner. Some, with their wares, came to trade. Some, tempted by the richness displayed in Svarṇabhūmi, sought service under the king. The generous king employed them intelligently. At the same time he saw to it that the people of his country lived in peace and prosperity.

Many were the conquests of Jayadeva. He was noted for his wisdom, thoughtfulness and courage. Though a lover of martial arts, he was by nature pious, God-fearing and righteous. Many were the temples built by this king. Under his benevolent care, worship was offered in the temples for the various deities in all splendour. The matins and vespers were periods when even a casual wayfarer there was wafted into a mood of ecstasy by the dulcet sounds emanating from the temples and bhajana maṇḍapas. The place seemed to beggar even the gay courtyard of Indra, the king of the Gods. In such splendour did king Jayadeva rule his land.

The vicissitudes of time do bring in their wake many changes. Years rolled by. The king became old. He was issueless. Yet, it did not worry him. He spent his time judiciously in serving his countrymen. Oftentimes he would be found in the mantrālaya, discussing with his wife and ministers ways and means to augment the coffers of his exchequer. In a kind and considerate way he would spend this wealth in building up a buffer stock of grains and foodstuffs needed for his countrymen during times of drought. By such thoughtful measures, he kept his people above want. The contented people in turn prayed for peace and prosperity for the king. But the wise ministers were able to perceive in the king a marked change. He was becoming more and more introverted. Gone was his gusto in martial arts. He spent less time in his pleasure arbours. Spiritual discourses engaged him more and more. All this betokened that he was preparing to welcome the messenger of death. The ministers got panicky.

One day, the ministers approached the king, and paying him their obeisance, with folded hands said, "Salutations to Your Highness. Please permit us to place before Your Highness our worry which, like a canker in the core, is eating us away." The king said, "How come that there should be, in my retinue, ministers with any worry? How is it that I was not aware of it all these days? Delay not. Speak of it immediately. I shall try to assuage, to my level best, your troubled souls". This heartening reply from the just king comforted the ministers and they, in unison, went on "Lord, we are happy, contented and above want, both materially and spiritually, thanks to Your Highness for your thoughtfulness and righteous rule. But if our Lord should leave us for the other world (God forbid), who will, so ably and efficiently, so justly and judiciously, so lovingly and thoughtfully, rule us thereafter? This country of ours has not been blessed with a prince to succeed Your Highness. This is our worry."

This request of the ministers produced a benign smile in the king. He said, "My beloved ministers, well do I see in eyes your concern for the country. Just is your demand. It is but meet that I should satisfy your demand. I shall myself choose my heir. He shall be wanting in nothing. He shall, I am sure, succeed me and continue to bear the beacon light of this mighty Svarṇabhūmi in all its might and majesty for many years to come." This reply surprised the ministers for they knew it was no easy task to choose a worthy heir for their unparalleled king. Yet they had enough faith in their king and they did not question him about how he would choose the heir.

The king got busy. He ordered his ministers to set up an exhibition in an extensive area. He gave them minute instructions as to what items of display ought to be housed in the exhibition. This fair, he said, he was arranging to choose his heir. He asked his ministers to go and announce to the people that he was giving them a chance to show their ingenuity. In the exhibition, somewhere in a chosen spot in the centre of some attraction, would he be. He who recognises him and identifies him in this exhibition would be chosen as the heir apparent. The king told the ministers that the stalls and booths should so tempt the people that only the strong willed, steadfast, prudent, painstaking and persevering individual would be able to identify him. With this end in view he made his ministers arrange the exhibition.

The exhibition was put up in an area of four square miles. Many were the stalls and varied were the booths. There were lotteries, shooting galleries, dancing halls, theatres, swimming pools, performing parrots, a craft section, an art section, sweetmeat stalls to satisfy the palate of one and all, and many other items on display. The exhibition ground with its resplendent banners, streamers and coloured festoons presented the appearance of a gaiety land. The place provided fun, frolic and mirth, not only to the young but also to the old. In one corner was built a temple. A tank with crystal clear water beautified the place fronting the temple too.

The exhibition was to be open from eight in the morning to eight in the night. It was to be there until the heir apparent was chosen. The magnificent glorious and resplendent exhibition attracted in tens of thousands the people of the country. From far and near came the throng to try their luck. The stalls were alluring, the booths enticing, the dancing halls tempting and the theatres enthralling. The gay show, with its gorgeous set-up, inveigled the people into enjoying the objects displayed. The comely sights that they saw, the melodious music that they heard and the delicious food that they ate freely there, transported them to a heaven of bliss unheard of in the annals of history. Caught up in such attractions, people forgot that they had gone there to identify the king and thereby become the heir apparent. Some who had a degree of patience, tried to see if they could identify the king in any of the people stationed in the stalls. So strenuous was this task that in the end they gave it up and took to enjoying the objects displayed there.

Two days passed without any favourable result. On the third day, a swain from a neighbouring village came riding a horse into gaiety land. Not willing to waste his time, he rode in on horseback with the only aim of detecting the king. With his subtle mind he sifted the sights that he saw and asked himself whether he could espy in any of these at least a semblance to the king. Though his mind was hitched to the goal of identifying the king, he did not despise the sights that he saw and the melody that he heard. Outwardly he seemed to enjoy everything that came his way, but his keen and incisive intellect was trying to descry, in and through the warp and woof of the beauty of the exhibition, the king in flesh and blood. But he too, seemed to lose heart. In vain he had searched in all places for the king. But the thought of the goal that he nourished constantly and continuously in the innermost recesses of his mind, released in him an extra quantum of energy to strive, to seek, to find and not to yield until the goal was reached. So he moved on and on. At last he came to the temple. This was the only place he had not searched. He had a holy bath in the temple tank. Then with due reverence he entered the temple. He went into the sanctum sanctorum. There, to his heart's content, he had the darśana of the deity of his heart. But he did not get the darśana of the king.

The swain began to contemplate. He felt that if the king was to be found at all, he should be found in the temple. Though he carefully went around the temple thrice carefully, he was not able to espy the king. His quiet mind soon urged him to examine minutely the walls of the sanctum sanctorum for a secret door or passage. Soon his eagle eye saw a square block in the wall with an embossed sculpture work wrought on it. So lovely and divine was the work that he was about to miss the sight of the projection (it was only slight) in the wall. Now he was there before it trying to remove the block. He had to use all his might. Slowly it was coming out. Without letting it fall, he made it slide down the wall. Lo! there was a secret passage. It was dark. He stepped into the pillared darkness, feeling his way with his hands. Soon he came to another stone structure. Here again he felt a projecting square block. Lifting it the same way, he slid it down the wall. Light streamed out from that place. It was indeed a lovely chamber illuminated wonderfully. In the centre of the carpeted floor was the golden throne. The king was seated majestically on it. In mute wonder the simple swain stood in silent adoration of the lord of his land. His store of destiny was greater than his ecstatic wonder. But soon recovering his senses he fell prostrate before the king, paying his respects. The king too felt happy, for God had ushered into his presence a worthy heir.

This world with its varied attractions is the exhibition. God is the ruler Jayadeva. It is God who has created this world. He has sent us into the world not only to enjoy its beauties but also to recognise that in the attractions of the world of objects, emotions and thoughts, we do not lose sight of our goal, the identification of ourselves with the Supreme. We can realise God if we act like the swain, with subtlety, steadfastness, patience and perseverance. We should not allow the objects of the senses to entice us away from our goal. At the same time we ought not to despise the world of objects. We ought to enjoy what comes our way, but should not become slaves of enjoyments. This is in short what the parable tells us.

9. The One In The Many

Jagannathan was a petty clerk in a local establishment which dealt in hardware. He was a man of infinite patience and indefatigable industry. Early in life, when he was twenty, his parents had yoked him to the cart of householdership, and in double blessedness he found his family becoming larger and larger. In a decade he became the proud father of half a dozen children. Grovelling under the burden of the expanding family, he plodded on and on up the ladder of accountancy, and soon found himself qualifying in commerce. But with the unending demands of a lovely wife, who measured her status by comparing it with those of the rich neighbours, and the demands of a brood of hungry children whose thirst for sweets, toys and trinkets seemed even to exceed the thirst of Ulysses for adventure, he found that the barn of plenty was not sufficient to balance his budget. Born in a Hindu family whose one qualifying trait is supreme patience, he bore the burden with a quiet poise ever believing that God would show a way out of his financial muddle.

Once he was in a jubilant mood, spending a happy time with his tiny tots. In a moment of unpremeditated expansion, which was a weakness into which he often gravitated, he told his kids that he would take them to the world fair in the city on the coming Saturday. The next week began with a whirlwind of intense activity for him. He found himself plunging fathoms deep into a mire of official records, receipts, vouchers, ledgers, daybooks, and so on, preparing five sets of accounts for his concern which needed them for its meeting of the Board of Directors. The thought of taking his kids to the fair had swung clean out of his mind.

But Jagannathan's wife, who had heard his promise to his children, taking it seriously, harped on it on and off and even when the children had forgotten, she reminded them of the proposed visit to the fair in a thousand subtle ways. If the youngest kid refused to take his bath on time, she would say, 'Look, if you do not go now to take your bath, I will tell daddy not to take you to the fair this Saturday.' To another kid she would say, 'If you do not do your exercises properly, I will ask your daddy to drop you from the party that is to go to the fair this Saturday.' At breakfast, lunch, tea and supper the topic of the trip to the fair became a convenient means which she would wield subtly to instill some discipline into their minds.

And the inevitable Saturday was fast approaching. The children too, were eagerly longing for it. Jagannathan who had quite forgotten what he had told his kids, was planning to have at least two sessions of cards with neighbours that Saturday evening. This he had planned as a means of diversion for his overworked brain. He longed for these noisy sessions of hilarious rumpus. But his dreams were shattered when the longed for Saturday arrived, because his wife had been keeping alive, in the minds of his kids, the thought of the visit to the fair!

That Saturday evening when Jagannathan came home planning to have a session of cards, he was surprised to be greeted and welcomed by his children in their best attire, all spruce, all spick and span, flaunting their bright faces. He wondered where they were going! He asked his wife where she was taking the children, for she too was dressed daintily. Pat came the reply from his wife, "How could you forget so quickly your promise? Did you not tell your kids you would take them to the world fair this evening? They are waiting for you to finish your tea quickly and take them." Jagannathan, who loved his children to a fault, soon comforted his soul which yearned to play cards and got ready to go with the children to the fair.

Travelling by two buses, jostling with huge crowds, the gay party reached the world fair. The colourful crescendos of eye-catching stalls in all their inveigling beauty tempted and teased their lusty onlookers. The senses dragged the mind into a maze of meandering enticements. The mind too got divorced from the intellect. The lone intellect watching painfully how it had been deserted, looked wistfully at the mind and its brood of senses. Any amount of appeal by the intellect seemed to be of no avail in the welter of the kaleidoscopic attractions at the fair. This was the condition of all the kids.

Just then Jagannathan saw a sweet vendor hawking his wares loudly before the children. Lowering the tray of sweets temptingly towards the children, he invited them to have a go at them. The situation was awful for Jagannathan. Perceiving that his purse was slender and that the demands of the children would go sky-high, he quickly guided his children out of the trap, pointing out to them the coloured fountain in the made-up lawn. But the father was no match for the sweet vendor. Wherever he went, the vendor dogged his footsteps. The children had spotted the sweets. Their mouths were fast salivating. They looked at the sweets wistfully. The older ones tugged at their father's coat demanding that he should buy them the sweets. The sweetmeats too, in lucent colours of gay carnation, purple, speckled gold, azure, amethyst, light lemon yellow, burning red, crimson and saffron; in shapes of beasts of the fields, birds of the air and creatures of the deep, perplexed the gazing kids that ranged around. The children, recognising the nodding gesture of permission from their father, crowded round the vendor and took out of the tray, the sweetmeat of their choice. One took a horse, another a lion, yet another a hawk, one a vulture, one a sparrow and the tiny tot the stag. The poor father, wishing to end this affair quickly, paid the vendor off, and soon led his kids away from the charms of the vendor.

But all was not well. The elder, who had chosen the lion, turning to the one who had the horse, said, "Look, mine would make mincemeat of yours, for mine is a lion, the king of the forests". Another who had a vulture, turning to the one who had a sparrow, teased him out of his wits telling him that his vulture would tear the entrails of the sparrow with its sharp beak and razor sharp talons. So the ones, who had chosen the weak ones, sore at heart, began to cry loudly, demanding that their father buy for them the stronger animals. Even the tiniest tot, a sweet nuisance of twelve months, holding his stag in his tiny fingers, cried non-stop demanding that he be given the one in the other child's hand. The fate of the householder is a matter for epic, a saga for a novel and a gingery grist for the philosopher. The unhappy father, not willing to be outwitted by fate, assembled the quarrelling throng on the same lawn and turning philosopher, asked all of them to taste their sweetmeat and know that all the sweetmeats were in essence nothing but sugar and sugar alone. When the kids, through constant licking, found that the sweetmeats dissolved, losing their shape and colour, leaving behind only a sweet taste, they understood that all was sugar and nothing but sugar, soon they forgot their differences and walked along with their father fully pacified, wending their way home.

Like the ignorant children who quarrelled among themselves for the diverse sweetmeats of varying shapes which in essence were all sugar and nothing but sugar, we too, steeped in ignorance, quarrel in this world for the objects of the senses, recognising only multiplicity and differences when all are nothing but the one Supreme.

Parables

Just as the sweetmeats, irrespective of their shapes and colours, flavours and prices, were all sugar alone, having sweetness alone as their essential nature, so too, the sparkle in the eyes, the smile on the face, the grin of an enemy, the harsh words of jealousy and the soft notes of love, nay, even heat and cold, success and failure, even men, animals, trees and inert matter, are all nothing but the expression of the ineffable, auspicious Supreme.

10. Please Turn Over

It was a Sunday in mid-summer. Rajanikanth was in his study browsing through the latest Reader's Digest. There seemed to be some noisy argument in the common room. He could clearly hear the shrill voice of his wife, Nalini, who was admonishing her son Kamath who had played his latest trick on his younger sister and made her weep. Kamath, who was too intelligent for a boy his age, was ever inventing new pranks. It was too difficult for Nalini to control the boy. Whenever she accused him of playing pranks, he would justify his acts by tracing sanction for it from the epics. So well had he learnt the epics that his mother was beginning to wish that he had not learnt them. If she tried to keep him engaged with some work or the other he would finish it off quickly and find time for new mischief. This time Nalini felt that the boy really needed spanking, and so, dragging him by the hand, she brought him into her husband's study. In a tone of dissatisfaction she said to her husband, "Look here! I do not know why the schools should not run all round the year. On holidays this pet son of yours becomes a veritable mischief monger. He is then a problem to me. Here he is, teasing Sham. See if you can keep him engaged, or else give him a good spanking so that he behaves himself". So saying, she left Kamath there and went back to the common room.

Rajanikanth looked at Kamath who was eyeing the carpet. His face was writ large with mischief. Perhaps the extra dynamism in him waited for a conducive field to express itself! Rajanikanth's eyes fell on the latest issue of The Economist, which was lying on the table. Suddenly, a wave of satisfaction passed through his mind. Taking the magazine in his hand, he flitted through the pages and calling his son, pointed to the central page and said, "Now Kamath, look at this world map for a while. Observe carefully the contours, I am going to scissor it off into several irregular segments and you will then have to piece them together to get back the world map. This will give you fun enough. Now take this, observe it for two minutes and return it." Kamath took the magazine and looked at the map. It was indeed very intricate. If scissored once, he knew it would be hell's work to piece it together again. The boy sat there looking at the map, lost in thought.

Rajanikanth once again began to pore over the pages of the Digest. The boy meanwhile, turned the page over. There flashed across his mind a gust of joy. He came back to his father and gave the map back to him. Rajanikanth now took the map and cut it into several irregular segments. Jumbling them up, he handed them over to Kamath and said, "Kamath take a sheet of paper and place on it these pieces and piece them together." Kamath took them eagerly and went to a corner of the room. Sitting on the carpet, he began arranging them well. In three minutes he was able to piece them all together. And now on the sheet was the original map all put together sprucely. He brought it before his father. Rajanikanth was astonished to see this feat, for he knew that even he could not have pieced them together even if he had been given half an hour's time. So he said, "Marvellous! Kamath, how did you ever do it? It is really a remarkable feat". Pat came Kamath's reply, "Daddy, it is all very easy. The map by itself would have given any guy, however intelligent or observant he be, a hell of trouble. But I turned the page over, and lo! on the other side I saw a full length picture of a man dressed up sprucely. It was an advertisement for Matador suitings. So, as soon as you gave me the pieces, I turned them over and bearing in mind the form of the man and the colour cavalcade, I pieced them together quickly." The father could not but marvel at the sagacity of his son.

The cosmos in which we live is a big jigsaw puzzle, intricate in design and enchantingly endless in variety. Knowledge is infinite and the time at our disposal is short. The more we uncover knowledge, the more do we see areas of darkness. This will be so in the outward march. This will be so with everything in this world. So to think of acquiring complete knowledge in this world through outward seeking is to ask for the impossible. But if one does wish to have it, there is really a way, say the Upaniṣads. They are not tired of roaring out their message, 'Know Thyself. Thyself shall reveal unto thee everything. Turn within.' Just as Kamath was able to piece together the world map by turning the page over and piecing together the figure of the man, so too, we should turn within and study the Self which is the very source of everything. It is the supreme Self 'Om', which being known, everything else becomes known. So, he who wants to know all about the world of OET (Objects, Emotions and Thoughts) should turn within and piece together his PFT (Perceiver, Feeler, Thinker) and direct it to abide in the very source 'Om'.

11. The Mirrored Hall

Maṇipāla was a mighty monarch of the Magadha kingdom. His glory had spread throughout India. This glorious king was fond of gay colours, and so enjoyed seeing himself dressed in pink or purple, carnation or azure, speckled gold or leafy green robes. His taste for colours was so subtle, that he could easily distinguish between any two hues of the same tint even if they were slightly and subtly different. There in his large and beautiful palace, was a mirrored hall which was the centre of attraction. Maṇipāla had made it a point to visit this hall every time he left the palace and every time he entered it. On such occasions he would stand before the mirrors and see reflected in them his myriad manifestations and get lost in the majesty and beauty of his handsome physique.

This monarch was a connoisseur of creatures and so had the best menagerie of pet animals. Among the pet animals that constituted his live collection was an Alsatian dog, huge in build and fierce in looks. Should a thought about this Alsatian flit through his mind, the monarch would order that it be brought to his august presence. He would then fondle it and feed it with choice butter biscuits and bars of chocolate. The dog too, had developed a taste for biscuits and chocolates of the finest kind and would not touch ordinary ones even with the longest bargepole.

One morning the monarch was attired gorgeously, for it was the day he was requested to inaugurate the big spinning mills recently installed by a group of wealthy tycoons of his country! On this occasion he had decided to wear an amethyst robe with carnation and gold tassels. His diadem was special, studded with choice stones of precious kind. A special streamlined car, in all its regal splendour, was waiting at the portico to take the monarch to the place of the inauguration. The monarch in his lustrous silken robes, as was his wont, entered the mirrored hall and stood there before the mirrors that adorned the walls, eyed his multiple reflections with a sense of fulfilment and then emerged out of the hall. His pet Alsatian dog, standing outside the mirrored hall was curious to see what the chamber contained. He translated his thought into action, and when he entered the hall, lo! there stood before him a myriad Alsatians of his own kind, looking at him with as much animosity and wonderment as he. Now the dog said to himself, 'Is this the secret? I thought I was his chosen pet. Now I see that he goes into this chamber to show my mettle to these creatures and prove my worth'. Stung with the green eyed monster of jealousy, he growled at them and gnashed his teeth. To his amazement, he found that all of them simultaneously growled at him and gnashed their teeth with as much vigour and abomination as he did. Now he could not contain his hatred for these creatures, and so pounced on them and began attacking them.

In the evening, the monarch overfilled with joy that he had successfully inaugurated the spinning mills, returned. Once more he went into the mirrored hall. There he found that all the mirrors had cracked at a height of three feet from the ground. There were blood stains on the mirrors. The monarch's ire was on the ascent. He was on pins and needles to know who the author of the mischief was. As he turned around, he saw in one corner his own Alsatian with all its teeth gone, with its sanguine jaws soaked in its own blood, lying unconscious in a pool of blood. Now he understood who was responsible for the tragedy in the mirror hall. The poor creature, his ill-fated Alsatian, instead of enjoying its myriad reflections, in its own ignorance, had become a victim of its own hallucinations and hence met with its fate.

The world in which we live is the mirrored hall. We, who are none other than the infinite Consciousness, are the monarch, but veiled by ignorance, we come to suffer the throes of agony and thraldom. Instead of enjoying our myriad manifestations in the world of plurality, we, like the dog, come to see in our own reflections, objects of hatred, sorrow and suffering. We ought to identify ourselves with our own supreme Self, then the mirrored hall will be an object of joy and enchantment, but if on the other hand, like the dog in our ignorance we come into this mirrored hall, we have to eke out only our quota of sorrow and suffering. Walk into the mirrored hall as a God and not as a dog.

12. The Beggar Turned King

He was poor and plebeian. His abode was a sheltered corner of the pavement. A patched up gunny, supported slantingly by two sticks descending from a point on the way side lamp post, was the roof of his little hut, nay, a travesty of a hut. The sides were covered with tin sheets and scrap iron picked up from the dustbins. The structure itself was an improvised one, but it was sufficient for the beggar against the inclemencies and vagaries of the weather. This beggar made his routine rounds in the streets of the town. In tattered clothes he would stroll casually, with a Dalda tin hung from his shoulders, eagerly expecting from the householders and the merchants, his dole of food and coins. A pie or two (for that was the coin of least value in circulation then) was all that he expected as charity from the shopkeepers. A busy day for the shopkeepers was a sad day for him, for they, in their hurry to transact business quickly, would fall foul in him and deny him anything when he appealed to them for charity. Such was the grovelling life the beggar had led for more than three decades, that hopes of a brighter future had completely vanished from his mind. With a resignation, unusual to a beggar he went about his way in the tortuous jungle of life. The shopkeepers, through constant recognition of the lot of this beggar, had come to develop a kindred interest in him, called him the beggar with the Dalda tin.

On days when the dole he received was good, he would feel in seventh heaven. On days he did not get anything, he would curse others, himself and his fate. Tossed like this from elation to dejection this beggar became a creature of circumstances. Great indeed was the potential difference between the fluctuations in the emotional graph of this beggar.

One day, as he was on his routine rounds, he saw a jeep honking loudly and coming to a stop near him with a screeching sound. Four liveried servants jumped out of the jeep and ran towards him. The frightened beggar took to his heels. But the liveried servants ran after him and caught hold of him. The beggar began to cry. He implored them to let him off, for he had not harmed even a fly, let alone committed a crime. But they would not leave him. They lifted him bodily on to a seat in the jeep. The beggar tried to release himself from them but in vain. The jeep started moving. The beggar panicked. Little did he know who they were, why they had caught him and where they were taking him. When he asked them, they said that he would know by and by. The beggar's only consolation was that he was neither bound to the seat nor beaten up or manhandled by the liveried servants.

The jeep stopped in front of a palace. The servants asked the beggar to get down. The beggar jumped out of the jeep. He was still holding in his hands the Dalda tin. The servants led him to a bathroom where they bathed him in scented water, scrubbed him clean and then dressed him in royal robes. Then they ushered him into the banquet hall where he was entertained with the tastiest of delicacies. With gusto the beggar began to gobble the food, for he had never tasted such victuals in his life. As he came out of the hall, he thought of his only possession, the Dalda tin, and so, ran back to the bathroom where he had left it. The servants too, ran after him. The moment the beggar saw his Dalda tin and the tattered clothes, he took them, but the servants who came after him forcibly removed them from him. The annoyed beggar said, "I say, why do you take away from me my only possession? I thank you for feeding me so well, but I do not know why you have taken away my Dalda tin and tattered clothes". The servants said, "Look here my dear man, a surprise is waiting for you, your star is in the ascendant. Have the goodness to contain yourself for a while and you will come to know why we are treating you like this". They then asked him to follow them. The beggar mutely followed them. They led him to the Darbāra hall, where the ministers, in colourful splendour, were anxiously waiting to receive the new heir to the throne.

As the beggar entered the hall, all the dignitaries stood up and paid their obeisance to this beggar in royal robes. The beggar was surprised, he thought it was all a make-believe. So he addressed them, "Sirs, I do not know why are you all bowing to me. You are driving me mad by curtsying like this." The Prime Minister said, "Your Majesty! You are the heir to the throne. Please honour us by ascending the throne". The beggar said, "You are mistaken. I am only a beggar. The servants here have forcibly brought me here. I am not your king, nor am I your king's heir. I am nothing but a beggar, plain and simple. Please allow me to go back to my place". The ministers said, "Your Majesty does not know his own lineage. You are the rightful heir to the throne. When our king died childless, we tried to trace his heir in the royal family. After a thorough investigation we found that a distant relative of the king's father, while on a pilgrimage with his wife and only child, was waylaid by highwaymen and robbed of their possessions and life. The child alone was spared. Leaving the child to his fate, the highwaymen disappeared. The child had on his person a mole on the right ear and a scar on the left ankle. Two days later, the king came to know from hunters under his pay the fate of his relatives. The bereaved king searched for the child, but the child was nowhere to be found. The king's efforts to trace the child were all in vain. When the king passed away without leaving any heir, we redoubled our efforts to trace the child, for he was the only heir. The clues that we had, led us to you. We were sorry to see you in the habiliment of a beggar. We could easily see on your person the mole on the right ear and a scar on the left ankle. It is really our good fortune that has brought the only one in the royal line back to us. So please deign to accept our offer and bless us by presiding over the destiny of this country".

Years passed. The beggar turned king had thoroughly transformed himself into a king. The onerous responsibility he had come to shoulder did not leave him any time to reminisce on his past. Things were moving smoothly in the country under his able rule. One day, as he was walking past a chamber, his eyes caught sight of a cupboard that was locked. He had not noticed it all these days. Just then he wanted to know what it contained. So he ordered his page to open it. He opened it. Lo! To his utter amazement, the king saw his Dalda tin and tattered clothes! A funny thought occurred to him and took complete possession of him. He did not want his ministers to know of it. So he locked the cupboard, took the key from the page and went to his chamber. He asked his page to leave him alone for a while. When the page had gone, the king came out, opened the cupboard, took out the Dalda tin and the tattered clothes and shoved them into a suit case. Then he called his minister-in-attendance and told him that he had some urgent business which he wanted to transact alone and so wanted none to follow him. He would return after twenty four hours. He came out. The chauffeur was at the wheel. The king beckoned the chauffeur and gave him a day's holiday telling him that he wanted to go alone, driving the car himself. Then, with his suitcase, he got into the car and sped towards the old town where he had been a beggar.

When he reached the outskirts of the town, he stopped the car, removed his royal robes, donned the beggar's clothes and stepped out into the street once again to play the part of the beggar for a while. Taking the Dalda tin and singing an old ditty he knew, he walked into the town. He found that the town had not changed much over the years. No one in the town had cared to find out where he had gone. But then when he made his appearance with the Dalda tin, they recognising him, asked him in surprise where he had been all these days. The beggar told them that he had gone to the next town to seek his fortune there, but not being successful, had returned to his old town. Little did the shopkeepers know that he was their very king. The beggar began his rounds through the streets of the town singing a ballad. Some, as was their wont, dropped some coins into the Dalda tin and some who were busy trading, vehemently poured their curses on him. The beggar was unaffected by anything that took place. He moved about even minded. He enjoyed the game to his heart's content. The extra dole given to him by the people there did not lift him to seventh heaven nor did the curses heaped on him make him feel dejected. Cushioned with the warmth of the thought that he was their very king who could, if he wished, confiscate all their property, he moved from shop to shop, house to house receiving happily whatever they gave him. He did not mind their curses nor the words of endearment they bestowed on him. Playing the part of a beggar happily, he returned the next day to his palace.

This parable tells us how a Man of Perfection, who has won over his mind and has come to experience the infinite Self, will no more thereafter feel any extra joy on receiving what is pleasant, nor grieve on receiving what is unpleasant. Just as the beggar turned king, when he came to experience his royal status, felt no upsurge of joy on receiving the dole of food or coins, nor any grief on receiving the curses, so too, a Man of Perfection, untrammeled by the whims and fancies of the people, moves about singing always the soulful song of the Infinite.

13. Renounce and Enjoy

Rama Sharma went on an official assignment to Washington D.C. In his short sojourn there, he happened to get close to Michael Drayton, his counterpart in the official machinery there. Having many things in common, they became bosom friends soon. When Rama Sharma's assignment in Washington was over, it was only with an unwilling heart that he took leave of Drayton. The latter too, felt that separation from his friend was painful. He told Sharma that he would take the first opportunity to come to India about which he had heard a lot but had not seen that country so far.

Months rolled by. Autumn came. An American Peace Mission Foundation was vigorously enlisting into its fold men of integrity, men who possessed a broad outlook and a catholicity of taste. Drayton found himself working for it heart and soul in Washington. This foundation wanted to carry the message of peace to all the countries in the East. Drayton was drafted into this group. On the very first lap of their journey, the team found itself alighting in Bombay. The team was accommodated at the Taj.

Sharma, and all that Sharma had said, were very much in the mind of Drayton. He remembered Sharma's commendation on the special savour of bananas. He had not tasted them till then. So, that morning he ordered a dozen bananas. In fifteen minutes, the attendant brought the bananas and laid them on a tray on the table. Drayton, who had heard from Sharma that they would taste extremely sweet, was very eager to eat them. He was only waiting for the waiter to depart. So when the waiter departed, he fell to eating the bananas. Soon he found that they were not as sweet as he had imagined them to be. The sourness which seemed to accompany the sweetness when he ate the bananas, made him doubt the words of Sharma. Drayton said to himself, 'Perhaps, to the Indians, these taste sweet, for they are habituated to this, but for me it does not suit.' He had only tried four of them. He refrained from eating the rest. With a sense of disappointment, he rang the bell. The waiter came. Drayton asked him to remove the plate. The waiter was puzzled. He looked at the plate and then at Drayton,

then at the plate and then at Drayton, three times. Drayton was unable to understand why the waiter was gazing at him that way. He thought that the Indian waiters lacked etiquette. Carrying the plate the waiter left the room. Drayton got busy with the Peace Mission.

A week later Drayton happened to go to Delhi. Sharma being in Delhi, Drayton called on him. Sharma received him warmly and in all enthusiasm asked him, "Mr. Drayton, did you taste our bananas? Are they not delicious?" Drayton's face fell. He said, "Well, Sharma, I did taste them but I am sorry, I do not have the Indian tongue to relish them. Perhaps you are the ones chosen by God to enjoy them".

Sharma, not to be so easily outwitted, said, "Look here Mr. Drayton, a banana is a banana whether it is for an Indian or an American. It must impartially yield the same sweetness to all, perhaps the ones you tasted in Bombay were unripe ones. I will now give you the finest ones. Taste them and tell me how delicious they are". Sharma asked his daughter to get the bananas. But the troubled Drayton said, "Mr. Sharma, please excuse me. I am sure I will not relish them". Sharma said, "Mr. Michael, the ones I have, are the choicest." You must enjoy them as I did. Now try this one". So saying, he thrust that one into his friend's hands. Unwillingly, Drayton began to eat it. But even now he experienced the same type of sourness he experienced at Bombay. Sharma looked at him. He could not contain his laughter. Michael felt puzzled. He said, "Mr. Sharma, why are you laughing at me? Is there anything funny in what I do?" Sharma still laughing, said, "Now I understand why you did not relish the bananas at Bombay. My dear man, there is a technique in eating also. Even here, you have to renounce and enjoy. Look at the way I eat it. You have to peel off the rind and eat only the pith. The rind will certainly taste sour. You chewed the banana with its rind and hence you did not enjoy its taste. You have to renounce the rind and enjoy the essence. This, indeed, is the technique in any enjoyment. Renounce the outer and enjoy the inner". Sharma now peeled off the rind and gave the pith to Drayton. Drayton tasted it. It was indeed delicious!

All of us come to suffer in the world in the same way as Drayton suffered. Just as he failed to renounce the rind, so too, we fail to renounce our clinging attachment to the world of objects. Hence, we fail to get the maximum enjoyment. We too squeeze out of every experience its content of joy. Alas! We find it is joy poisoned with sorrow. The art of detachment alone, while doing work, can confer on us the unadulterated peace and joy. Hence the scriptures say, 'Renounce and Enjoy'. 'Tena tyaktena bhuñjīthā mā gṛdhaḥ kasya-sviddhanam' – Īśāvāsya-upaniṣad.

14. The Anchorite and The Malacca Cane

Sadhu Jagadish was an anchorite, not by choice but by necessity. He had taken to this calling not because he had any immortal longings, nor a burning desire to liberate himself from the thraldom of perennial plurality, but because he found that this way of life suited his extreme inertia and indolence. His was a simple hut on the banks of the Ganga. Blessed by the Lord with a good physique, he had a lustrous glow about himself when clothed in ochre robes. The glow with which he was invested, made even a casual passerby take him for a devout soul well advanced in yoga. But who knew that he had taken to this calling to satisfy his belly? He toiled neither physically nor did he bend his mind towards the taste of self-control. The clear stream of the Ganga slaked his thirst and the charity of gullible pilgrims served to fill his belly. Enviable indeed was the position of this sadhu!

That was a day of festivity. A pilgrim from the south who had wended his way to this sacred city chanced to see this anchorite. Since the pilgrim had come there to expiate the sin of having deceived his own kith and kin and since he felt that an anchorite was worthy of worship, he decided to give Sadhu Jagadish a generous offering of a ten rupee note, a saffron coloured dhoti and an upper cloth into the bargain. These he gave to the anchorite and as was the custom, he gave him a cup of gingerly oil too with which the anchorite was expected to anoint himself and have a bath. The anchorite accepted these and blessed the pilgrim in return.

The anchorite, having put away the ten rupee note, securely safe from all prying eyes, anointed himself with the oil from head to foot, plunged into the Ganga and had a pleasant bath. Then he donned the new dhoti and the upper cloth given to him by the pilgrim. The pilgrim then fed him with nice delicacies that he had brought with him. Having obtained the blessings of the sadhu, the pilgrim returned home supremely satisfied. His hunger and thirst having been appeased, this anchorite amused himself by seeing the play of light and shade on the waters that meandered musically down the river.

As the anchorite was satisfying his idle curiosity, he saw a bright object floating down the stream. He did

not wait to consider the situation. Down he plunged into the river and with deft strokes swam straight towards the shining object and with a gleeful gasp caught hold of it. Then lifting it out of the waters, he saw that it was a Malacca cane with a silver handle. As he was thinking of his good luck, he did not notice that the current was taking him down the stream. Now he turned back, and with the cane in one hand, started swimming back. But all was not well with him and the cane. 'Man proposes and God disposes.' It was at this very moment, as he was thinking of his good luck, that he found himself caught up in a dangerous whirlpool. The more he strove to come out of the vicious current, the more it sucked him to its centre. The anchorite desperately fought with the current. Only one hand of his was free to help him as the other held the cane. Now, his instinct of self-preservation gained the better of his greed, and so, loosening his hold on the cane he kicked himself out of the whirl. The cane, thrown away with force, was floating down the stream. The anchorite reached the bank.

Then he saw the cane floating down the stream, far away from him. Unable to bear the loss, he began to wail and weep saying that he had lost his cane. Another sadhu who was all the while watching this panorama, said to him, "Jagadish, a few minutes back when you were on the banks of the Ganga, you had no cane. The cane that floated down the stream would have continued its course if you had not disrupted its course. You, driven by your greed, plunged headlong into the water, caught hold of the cane and claimed it as yours. Later, when you lost your hold on it while freeing yourself from the whirlpool, you did not strive to get it. Now that you are safe on the banks, you say you have lost your cane. In what way is the cane yours? Is not all this sorrow of your own choosing? Give up this unholy attachment to that which is not yours".

Like the anchorite, we too, in our ignorance, whipped by the forces of greed and desire, come to maintain a wrong relationship with the world of objects, emotions and thoughts. We come to lay waste our powers, running pantingly after the objects we wish to possess, and thereafter, madly wrestle to preserve these objects, forgetting the truth that everything in the world obeys the law of movement and change. The world is in a continuous state of flux, and he who comes to disturb the harmony of this movement, comes to reap his quota of pain and sorrow. Welcome all those that come towards you, stand not in the way of those that are leaving you. 'Āgatam svāgatam kuryāt, gacchantam na nivārayet.'

The objects in themselves have no power to give us pain or pleasure. We, through our attachment with the objects, invest them with power to throw us out of gear, to exhilarate us or depress us.

15. Food Poisoning

Kittu's results were out. He was in seventh heaven, for on that day he had distinguished himself head and shoulders above his classmates in the school final examination! His mother, in the deep recesses of her mind, was offering her thanks to the Almighty for having successfully answered her prayers. Her mind moved ahead in time to meet the future. Ten years of plodding penury had sapped her, and it was only her will that had sustained her. She would now ask her son Kittu to seek a job in Madras. Raman, her first son who was in Madras, was struggling to make both ends meet with his meagre income as a steno in a firm in the city complex. Though endowed with a heart of gold, which flowed out in a mercurial kindness to help his mother out of the woods of abject penury, yet he did not possess the golden Midas touch. Thither did the mother think of sending Kittu.

Letters had already been written to Raman to be on the lookout for a job for Kittu. That evening Kittu was off to Madras. He was received at the bus stand by his brother. Soon he found himself in the house of his brother Raman and his wife. She, it seemed to Kittu, was not happy over this additional burden on her family. Yet she appeared to do what she could to stretch the resources to meet the demands of all three of them there. Days passed. Kittu, who had come with a rosy vision of his future, was slowly getting disillusioned. God he knew, but godfather he had none! His brother Raman had pressed him into the pattern he himself had gone through, to learn typewriting and shorthand. Kittu was not averse to it, nay, he was willing to do anything that would find him a job.

Kittu, who, right from the moment he arrived in Madras, had entertained the notion that his sister-in-law was not well disposed towards him, saw in everything she did, some unjust and subtly directed attack against him. This he had come to feel from the bottom of his heart. Three gruelling months had hardly passed when Kittu found himself a victim of a paroxysm of stomach ache. He felt that this had happened because his sister-in-law was mildly poisoning his food. When he could no longer bear the pain, he complained to his brother, who immediately took him to a good doctor. With love for his wife on the one hand, affection for his brother on the other, Raman did not know what to do. So he anxiously waited for the doctor's diagnosis. The

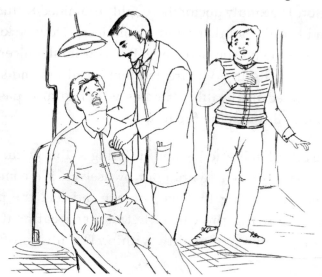

doctor who was apprised of the suspicion that Kittu entertained, examined the contents of the viscera, and to his amazement he did find the contents poisoned. He gave Kittu a course of medicine and said he would be all right.

Kittu was put on a diet and made to take the course of medicine. Still, Raman, who felt that his wife would not stoop to such underhand dealings, wanted to test his wife. The fact that the food was poisoned haunted him like a ghost. The next day he and Kittu sat together to eat. When the food was served in the plates and his wife had gone into the kitchen to fetch the other dishes, he surreptitiously switched the plates. If really the food had been poisoned, he should also suffer from the same complaint that day. He ate. Kittu too did eat. Raman did not get the pain even after five hours, but Kittu was already writhing in pain. His wife, he felt, after all was not to blame. Again with Kittu he rushed to the doctor. This time too, the doctor found the contents of the viscera poisoned. Raman explained the whole situation to the doctor. The kindly doctor thoroughly examined Kittu. Lo! he found Kittu's mouth a cauldron of ulcers. Now he knew from where the poison had come. It was from the ulcers in Kittu's mouth itself. So he treated him for ulcers and soon Kittu regained his health. Raman's wife had also passed successfully through the fire test.

We are all in life acting and suffering as this Kittu. The cause of our sorrow is within our ownselves. We come to envenom everything that we contact and feel the pain of it, not knowing the cause. Let us get treatment for the ulcers of our personality within. The ulcers of the volcano of vāsanās sending out their lava of poisonous desires contaminate the mind, which comes to alight on the world of perceptions through the organs of the senses and hence we come under the burden of the apparent unending sorrows of saṁsāra. Empty thyself of the ulcerous contents by exposing thyself to the benign influence of the white heat of meditation and enjoy the peace that sweetens all activity.

16. The Marwari Merchant

Gulabachand, a Marwari merchant, had by his indefatigable industriousness, raised himself to plutocratic heights in the lucrative field of export-import business. Blessed with extraordinary speculative powers, possessing critical acumen and aided by a sharp intelligence, this merchant directed his rich investments only in those channels that brought him rich dividends. Much to the chagrin of the other competitors in his line, he outbid the others in all business transactions. Being a man of the world, through prudent measures he had worked his way into the network of government gimmicks. Many were the officials who vied with one another to please this business tycoon by tipping him off about the latest budgetary moves contemplated upon by the cabinet members. This was the period when his stars were on the ascent. He was elected Chairman of the Chamber of Commerce.

Once, during an official visit to one of his several business establishments, as was his wont, he had to stay in a five-star hotel. That night, as he was cozily dozing off, he had a queer feeling that a bug had made its way into his ear, and hence into the brain. Gulabachand rang the bell, called the establishment's best doctor and apprised him of what had happened. He tried in vain to remove the bug by syringing it out. So Gulabachand had to go and consult several other doctors, all of whom were unable to cure him of his agony.

Gulabachand lost his peace. He could feel the bug moving every fifteen minutes, trying to settle itself in a more edible portion of his brain.

Gulabachand travelled from place to place, calling on various doctors of repute. Many were the experts who came, gave him injections, pills, potions, triturations, and so on. But none of these could reduce even a wee bit of his agony. None of the famous specialists, renowned surgeons, not even the famed one in Unānī, Homeopathy, Siddha or Āyurveda experts could give him relief.

Days dragged on. When he had almost become a neurotic patient, Karan Singh, a friend of his, recently returned from London, told him of an Indian surgeon, who had made a mark in London and returned to India and was appointed as the Chief Director of the Lucknow Government Hospital, could perhaps help him. So Gulabachand went to this Lucknow specialist. This specialist with all care and

attention, examined Gulabachand elaborately. Reserving his opinion, the doctor told the troubled patient that he would try his best to bring relief to him.

Gulabachand was hospitalized in a special room of the hospital complex. He was given V.I.P. treatment. In spite of all the medical attention he received, he was restless. He began to rave hysterically at nights. He was sleepless with excruciating pain which seemed to eat into his nerves bit by bit. When he was about to give up hope, a silver lining appeared on the cloud of his fate. The doctor rushed into the room one day with a sheaf of pamphlets in his hand, told him that if the businessman could send a man to the Western front, where the Indian soldiers were treated, he by using his influence, could procure for him a special medicine prepared by the Germans. He promised Gulabachand that, that medicine would certainly cure him of his agony. Any expense, if it could only relieve him of his agony, was cheap for the merchant.

A messenger was sent. Days passed. There was no sign of the messenger's return. In the meantime, despair and hopelessness were choking the merchant. One day, the messenger returned with the parcel. The doctor uttered a cry of joy, and opening the parcel, he showed the troubled patient the three vials that were in it and said, with all enthusiasm, "Here is the medicine! Now the miracle will happen! With these vials I can work wonders. With one I shall make the bug in your brain swoon. With the second, injected after a week, I will kill the bug and the third when administered after another week, will make the dead bug come out of the ear".

The merchant was beside himself with joy and felt extremely hopeful. The doctor told him that he would give him the first of the injections the next day. An air of excitement filled the hospital staff. The operation theatre was the scene of high drama. The doctor, aided by four other experts, surrounded by nurses holding the surgical instruments, administered the first of the injection to Gulabachand. Two hours passed. The patient then regained consciousness. He could feel, with a sense of relief, the effect of the injection. The bug in his brain had really swooned! That night, for the first time in many a month, he slept soundly. But on the third night the bug was up once again, creeping and crawling, screwing and burrowing and seeking a cozy and edible portion of his brain. The satanic bug! Four more restless nights passed.

Again the operation theatre was a scene of bustle and excitement. The second of the series of injection was administered. The Lucknow doctor had truly killed the bug. After sometime, the patient could really feel relief. He thanked the doctor profusely. Throughout that week, not once was the patient disturbed by the carcass of the bug inside his brain.

The first day of the following week was very auspicious for the Marwari merchant. The hospital wore a new look. The final year students of the medical college were called. They were given the special privilege of witnessing the famous doctor administering the third and final injection. All the elaborate precautions required for this strange injection of the costliest and rarest of German medicines, were taken faithfully. The last of the injections was administered dexterously by the Lucknow doctor. All eyes were focussed on the ear of the patient. Half an hour passed. The doctor washed the ear of the patient, and lo! floating in the water, in the basin was the dead bug! The doctor lifted the bug with a pair of forceps and held it up to the gaze of the satisfied and contented patient. The patient was wheeled out of the operation theatre.

The medical college students were wondering why they were asked to witness a mere injection! As if to satisfy their curiosity, the Lucknow doctor went to the door and after closing it carefully, wheeled round and faced them. "Friends" he said, "You have witnessed so far the cure of a very painful disease, for which the patient could not get a cure anywhere in the world. I will tell you frankly that the strange German vials are nothing but tubes of distilled water which I had procured from a local chemist around the corner of the street. The most difficult part of the operation was the hunt that I had to make for a live bug last night! When I got one at last, I pressed it carefully between my fingers in one end of my handkerchief and preserving the dead carcass, with a sleight of hand, I dropped it into the ear of the patient before washing the ear. The dead bug you saw coming out of the ear was this bug! Friends, maybe the means are unfair, but for an unreasonable patient's imagined disease, the only cure can be to take medicines with mere attributed powers!"

Viewed spiritually, all of us are also living the delusions of the merchant. We are suffering from the pangs of an imaginary 'bug' in us. This bug is the ego. Identifying ourselves with the ego, we come to entertain the wrong notions of I-ness and my-ness, agency and enjoyership and the consequent sufferings, sorrows, limitations, finiteness, and so on. Now we need a Lucknow doctor who will kill this ego sense, with the rare medicine of Ātmajñāna, the knowledge of the Self, which, when its purpose is served, shall be recognised as nothing new or rare, but as our own real nature!

17. The Vivacious Lady and The Mysterious Box

It was a day of hectic activity in Madras. The central station was a scene of colourful crescendos. The crowd gathered there consisted of people of different sorts. Some had come to see their friends off, some their relatives and some to pass their time sightseeing. The station seemed to take on a festive look. Just then a young gentleman, teeming with vim, vigour and vitality, headed towards a first class compartment. A porter followed him, deposited his luggage in the compartment, received his wage and disappeared in the throng there. The young gentleman, seating himself comfortably on the cushioned seat, began reading the latest issue of the Illustrated Weekly. As he was scanning the pictures with the deftness of a connoisseur, he looked out. There, on the platform, was a vivacious young lady bewitchingly beautiful. Clad in silken finery, flaunting an alluring smile and blessed with grace and elegance, she was the cynosure of attraction. This lady boarded the same compartment in which was seated the young man.

In speechless wonder, the young man looked at her wondering whether she was a fairy come down to earth. The Illustrated Weekly fell from his hands. In mute wonder he gazed at her. She was followed by a porter carrying a huge box of unusual dimensions. The lady, again smiling at the young man, said in a sweet and alluring tone, "Sir, if you do not mind, I shall keep this box here". The porter then carefully lowered the box on to the floor of the compartment and left. The lady once again favoured the young man with a smile and in a trice left the compartment and disappeared in the melee that had gathered there.

The young man, expecting to have a pleasant journey with the exceedingly beautiful lady, hoped she would take the seat opposite his. Now he looked at the huge box. Though the box was occupying a lot of space depriving his legs of free movement, admiration for the vivacious young lady made him bear with the inconvenience caused. The box set him musing. 'Perhaps the lady has gone to Higginbothams to get some magazines to relieve her of the tedium of the journey. By the by, what does the box contain?' A sweet perfume emanating from the box tickled his nostrils. 'Perhaps in the box was the entire ensemble of her apparel and jewellery', he thought.

Time passed. The first bell rang. The lady did not return. The young man began to wonder whether she, like the modern youth, was fond of boarding the train in motion. The second bell too rang. The guard blew the whistle and waved the green flag .... chick .... chick. .. fuff. .. fuff... The train steamed out of the platform. The young man was in a fix. His heart missed a beat. 'Why had the lady not come? Was she held up somewhere? What had happened to her?' Soon, his sagacious brain consoled him. Perhaps she was one of those modern ladies who missed a train only to have the thrill of speeding by car to catch the train at the next station! His mind was filled with sweet thoughts of the enchantingly beautiful lady. He lost count of the time. The train came to a halt at the next station. He went out. There was no sign of the lady coming.

Two gentleman in dark gray suits boarded the compartment. They came in and noticed the huge box. The young man also got in and took his seat. The two gentleman surmising that the box belonged to him, turned towards him and said, "Sir, why don't you transfer this box to the luggage van? Is it not an inconvenience to the passengers?" The young man replied, "What does it matter if it is here? If you want, you can stretch your legs on it". This answer lent credence to their surmise that the box was his. The train was on its onward march. The young man looked at the box. The more he looked at it, the more did his attachment for the box grow. The lady had not turned up. The train halted at two more stations and had picked up four more first class passengers. Yet, the lady had not turned up. This set the young man thinking.

The passengers were murmuring that the box was causing them a lot of inconvenience. But the young man, infatuated with the vivacious lady, did not feel the inconvenience. Now his mind began to ponder on what he should do with the box. Naturally, the box would contain the invaluable treasures of the lady. If the lady did not turn up, why should he not take the box with him? Now his train of thoughts was interrupted by the appearance of the ticket examiner. Having checked the tickets, he looked at the huge box and asked them whose it was. All the passengers, without a trace of doubt, in one voice said that it belonged to the young man. The examiner politely asked the young man to produce the luggage ticket. When the young man said that he did not have one, the examiner asked him whether the box had been weighed and booked. The young man said, "What if it has not been weighed?" Then the examiner said, "Sir, in that case you will have to pay Rs. 27.80 towards the luggage charges; shall I make a receipt, Sir?" The young man nodded. The examiner made a receipt, the young man paid him the amount, quietly received the receipt and stuffed it into his pocket. The ticket examiner got down at the next station. The young man's destination was two stations ahead. As the lady had not turned up, and inasmuch as she had not relayed any message either, he decided to take the box with him.

His destination came and the train halted. The young man hailed two porters and bade them carry the huge box. He was making his way towards the exit. A customs officer, who was passing that way, happened to see the unusually huge box. Interrupting the young man, he asked him to declare the contents of the box. When the young man looked sheepishly at him, he asked him if the box was really his. The young man produced the luggage receipt and said it was his. Now the officer wanted him to open the box, as he wanted to make sure he did not carry with him contraband goods. Now the young man, growing all the more sheepish, said that he did not have the keys. The suspicious officer then said that in that case the young man should follow him to the police station where the box would be opened and examined.

They reached the police station. The lock was fast and secure, and it was difficult for them to break it open. So they sent for a locksmith. The locksmith came with his tools and unlocked it. All the people there were eager to see what the huge box contained. The young man's eagerness was the most, as he also did not know what it contained. He expected to see costly jewellery and finery inside the box. The police officer opened the box. Lo! everyone there uttered a cry! The young man exclaimed, "Oh! What a folly!" What did they see inside the box? There lay a dead body, heavily scented. Now the young man said that the box was not his. He told the officer how a young, vivacious lady had come and deposited the box in the compartment and disappeared. But the police officer and the customs officer were not prepared to accept his explanation, because earlier the young man had declared that the box contained his wife's apparel and jewellery.

Added to this, he had unmistakably produced the luggage ticket too. His continued and frantic denial that the box was not his, fell on deaf ears. The young man was arrested, hand cuffed, and sent to prison. He had to stay there for four days before bail could be moved. After the bail, he had to prove his innocence in a court of law. It was a sore task for him and his lawyer. Though now he stoutly disclaimed the box, the circumstantial evidence was strongly against him. The mysterious box seemed to hold on to him. It seemed to claim him. Even if he tried to sever his relation with the box, the box stuck fast to him, as it were. After several months of litigation, producing all possible evidence of his innocence, he was released. But in so doing he had lost a good part of his wealth and his good name.

Jīva, the soul, on its journey through life, is the young gentleman. Māyā (the unmanifest or ignorance or nescience) is the bewitchingly beautiful vivacious lady. Māyā places at the disposal of the soul, the body. The body is the huge mysterious box. It is māyā that has produced the body through the pentamerous combination of the rudimentary elements. Now the soul, through its association with the body, propelled by the inherent power of māyā, claims the body as its own and comes to suffer the throes of thraldom. When the soul comes to know that the body is insentient and of no value (through the teachings of the Master) and that it (the soul) is only the pure Self, it tries to disown the body. But the body claims the soul as it were and does not leave the soul so easily. The soul will have to fight strenuously, seriously, industriously and intelligently for its release, just as the young man did in a court of law. This is the condition in which all of us are placed. We are in bondage. Having passed through the thraldom of existence through countless births we have come to believe that we are the body. Now, when the scriptures and our Masters say that we are not the body but the pure Self, we want to drop the idea that we are the body, but the body identification does not leave us, as it were. Such is the travail through which we pass.

18. Space Birds

In outer space lived two divine space birds, in all amity, companionship and cooperation. They led a blissful life, nurtured and nourished by the warm rays of the sun and the soothing rays of the moon. Age did not wither nor custom stale their infinite happiness. These birds were endowed with the power to live as long as they liked and to end their manifestation at will. For them, days danced in ecstasy and night in beatitude. Time sported and in due course these birds came to be possessed by the thought that they should perpetuate themselves in their offsprings. So, surrendering to the Almighty, they began courting.

The thought of perpetuation gained momentum and, blessed by the Almighty, they laid a number of eggs in space. These eggs, sparkling white and pearl-like in appearance, began dancing in space like lovely particles of scintillating stars. The parent birds were beside themselves with joy at the sight of their brood. The mother bird flew round and round them, eagerly and anxiously watching them. Every change in the eggs produced a flutter of joy in her. But the father bird, though drawn to his brood by love, though sharing silently every emotion of the mother bird, mentally maintained a sense of detachment. Blessed with a maturity of mind and endowed with a sense of equanimity, he knew that it would be a sore task to save the entire brood and hence dispassionately insulated himself against any dire consequences.

The mother bird flitted here and there, wondering why there was a delay in the eggs getting matured. As the days passed, the eggs hatched. They gradually lost their lustrous appearance and began developing cracks. From thousands of eggs the chicks shot out their bald heads and in unison began chirping. This disturbance in silence was as the music of the spheres to the mother, and she, in rapt attention, listened to the childish treble of its brood, silently offering homage to the Almighty for blessing her with such satisfaction. The young ones who had their entire structure, except the head, inside the shell, began enjoying the exciting experience. They welcomed the change for they felt that this experience was better than the one inside the shell. Snug and warm inside the shell, the chicks found their mother bird hovering around them, felt drawn to her. But they did notice a marked difference between their anatomical structure and that of their mother. Their mother had no shell as they had and they had not the wings, feathers and legs. They felt that their mother, with these unnecessary appendages, was more vulnerable as compared to them who were barricaded within the fortress of the shell. The varied experience that they were having prevented them from coming closer to their mother. The mother bird who in, her fondness for her brood, wanted them to come closer and get nourishment, felt that with the passage of time, the children would get tired of their newborn experience and turn to her. All the while, the father bird acted only as a witness, watching everything from the tower of his serene silence; but ready to render any assistance when needed.

The waves of eggs now were drifting in a definite direction. The parents, who had themselves been often wafted in different directions many a time by the whims and fancies of space, felt that this was one such phenomenon. But actually it was not so. The mass of eggs seemed to be descending towards

the fringe of the earth's gravitational field. Their descent seemed to be steady. The dispassionate father bird was able to observe this and soon communicated to his partner the news of the significant change in the descent. The mother bird, in turn commanding all the sweetness in her store, tried to warn her children in gentle terms of the possible danger of getting sucked in by the earth's gravity. The mother said, "Children dear, children dear, listen to me, your mother. Harken to me. We are divine birds and should fly freely in space, singing the song of the Infinite. Freedom consists in coming out of the shell. Nothing untoward will happen to you if you come out of the shell. You will gain your full freedom. Therefore kick the shell, close the eyes and spread the wings."

The brood of chicks in their sleek comfort felt within the shell, looked blankly at her. The mother, finding that her children had not understood her, with utmost concern for the brood, said again in a tone of ringing sincerity, "Children dear, please kick the shell, close the eyes and spread your wings, or else you will be sucked in by gravity". Some of the chicks hearing this, questioned the mother, "What if we are sucked by gravity? What can gravity do to us who are in warm comfort inside the shell? Further, how do you know that gravity is sucking us?" The mother answered, "Children dear, this is not the time for explanations. You know I am your mother. I will not deceive you. Please listen to me. It is in your own interest that I am asking you to do this, there is no time to waste, please kick the shell, close the eyes and spread your wings".

One of the chicks said, "We do not know for certain whether we have wings". Another said, "When eyes can show such fine sights, why should we close our eyes?" Yet another said, "Look here, comrades, do not listen to this bird's words. Were we not in cosy comfort inside the shell before we darted our heads out? Now don't we feel the cold lashing on our face? At least the body is snug and warm inside the shell. So why should we kick the shell? It will only be an act of indiscretion". The other chicks agreed with him. The mother, despairing at the false philosophy of the chicks, appealed fervently once again, to its children to follow her advice. Two chicks, just then, getting tired of their embryonic existence inside the shell, kicked their shells, closed their eyes and tried to spread their wings. In the beginning they did fall, but soon the wings spread and they began to float. The father bird, all the while at a distance, darted near these two birds and soon taught them how to use their wings and bade them to follow him. The two birds, excited by their experience, followed their father and flew up.

The mother in the meanwhile, wailing and weeping, again and again pleaded with her brood, "Children dear, do you not see that the speed of descent is increasing? Please follow my advice. See what the other two of your group have done. Follow their example." But the heedless brood, immersed in their own gossip, did not care to listen to their mother. The father bird, finding the mother bird and her brood in dire danger of being drifted away by the powerful force of gravity, shouted, "Dear partner, come quickly or you too will perish. You have done your best advising them what they should do. They do not listen to you. Leave them to their lot and ascend." The mother bird, with a pang of sorrow too deep to be swept away, painfully ascended the skies, now and then turning back to see her brood descending to their doom. The heedless brood, soon sucked by gravity, dashed to the earth and met with their doom. The parents with the two young ones ascended the skies and allured to brighter worlds led the young ones up. As days passed, they felt the urge to end their manifestation and so, slowly shedding their grossness, faded into nothingness, leaving their young ones to carry on their mission in life.

Those of us under the spell of ignorance are the brood of the space birds. Our scriptures and our spiritual Masters, like the mother bird, advise us to give up the idea that we are the body, mind, intellect (kick the shell), withdraw ourselves from our preoccupations with the unreal, impermanent, evanescent, temporal and transient world of objects, emotions and thoughts (close the eyes) and spread the wings of imagination born out of our insight into the scriptures and giving up the sense of difference, meditate on these truths and fly into the beyond to become one with the supreme Consciousness (spread your wings).

19. That Thou Art

Vishnu Varma, sipping leisurely a steaming cup of coffee, browsed through the newspaper. His eyes caught sight of an insertion in the obituary column which read, "Shridhara Varma, the business tycoon of Rangoon, reached the feet of the Lord yesterday". Only a week back, Vishnu Varma had met Shridhara Varma in Rangoon. He was then hale and healthy and there was no indication then that he would meet with his end so soon. He and Shridhara had been bosom friends for more than two decades. Vishnu Varma began to reminisce.

Shridhara was then unemployed. He had not learnt any trade or craft, but was on pins and needles to go into work. Just then he happened to meet a group of adventurous merchants on their way to Rangoon. He sought service under them. They too, finding him pliant, obedient, resourceful and enterprising, employed him. Thus Shridhara found himself in Rangoon running errands for these merchants and assisting them in their commercial transactions. Blessed with keen powers of observation and a nimble wit, he soon learnt the mechanics of commerce. Being a lone soul with no one dependent on him, this thrifty lad carefully saved what he could. By his kind disposition, gentle manners and cheerful appearance, he endeared himself to one and all there. The merchant community was kindly disposed towards him, for he never took to hot and rebellious liquors or wooed with unbashful forehead the means of weakness and debility. It was at this time, that one of the merchants from India wanted to wind up his business, sail home and spend his lusty winter on the soil he was born. This was an opportune moment for Shridhara and he bought up the business from this merchant.

The training he had received under the merchants, supplemented with his sagacity and resourcefulness, soon helped him to take giant strides in the field of business. Soon, he began to amass wealth. In his hands wealth shone, for, he made wealth serve him and the community. Being pious by nature, he spent a decent portion of his profit in charitable acts. The goodness of fortune smiled on him and he rose in status and soon became a millionaire. Though many a merchant offered his daughter in marriage to Shridhara, he declined politely and determined to live in single blessedness. Such was the eventful career of Shridhara Varma. Now Vishnu Varma remembered that only a week earlier Shridhara had written his last will and testament, naming his nephew as his heir. Vishnu Varma felt sad that he had lost his dearest friend.

His train of thoughts was interrupted by a young man who said, "Good day to you Sir, I hope you remember me. I am fed up with life in Trichy. I am here now hunting for a job. Though I am doing it with all the energy I can command, somehow it is eluding me. Disappointment coupled with despair seem to grin at me now. I know not how to tide over the crisis. I am tired and worn out. Thirst and hunger are driving me mad now. Please relieve me of the twin monsters. At present, all I need is a rupee or two". This emotional outburst from the young man touched the chords of kindness in Vishnu Varma. He looked closely at the young man. In surprise he uttered, "Ay, sonny, are you not Nandi Varma? It ill behoves you to ask me for a rupee or two, for now you are a millionaire". The bewildered lad, exasperated, cried, "Sir, Sir, this is not the moment for you to tease me. I know for certain I am poor and a plebeian. If, with myself I hold intelligence, or have acquaintance with my own past, if that I do not dream, then dear Sir, never so much as in a thought unborn did I claim to be a millionaire. Please take pity on me and help me. May God bless you"!

Vishnu Varma, patting Nandi Varma on his back, said, "Take heart, man, counsel patience. Do you not know what has happened?" The impatient lad, who had by now lost all his energy, said "Sir, tell me whether you are going to help me or not. Hunger and thirst are driving me mad". Vishnu Varma said, "Sonny, are you not the nephew of Shridhara Varma who left for Rangoon two decades back? Are you not his only heir?" The impatient lad burst forth, "What of it, of what avail is it now? He is miles and miles away and here I am struggling to keep the wolf out of the door". Vishnu Varma said, "Just are the ways of God and just His decrees, Nandi. Perhaps you are not aware of what has happened. Here is today's newspaper. See for yourself what it says. Your uncle passed away yesterday. He had named you as his heir in his will. Now you are a millionaire. So give up this cringing and fawning."

For a moment Nandi stood there dumbfounded. He was unable to believe his ears. Was his uncle, with whom he had never spoken more than two or three words at any time, so thoughtful and condescending as to make him his heir? Was it possible? But here it was and Vishnu Varma was there lending credence to it. Soon regaining his composure, he said, "Sir, I am beside myself with joy. May the heavens be praised. Now I do not need a rupee or two but a couple of thousands and your help to establish my rights in Rangoon. Though now I have the knowledge that I am the inheritor of my uncle's vast wealth, I am not a millionaire until I go to Rangoon, claim

my right, show my credentials and establish my kindred relationship with my uncle. Let all this wait. First please give me food and drink and help me. I shall requite you well for all this you do unto me."

Vishnu Varma got busy. He took a personal interest in Nandi Varma now. The love he bore for his friend made him stand by Nandi Varma now in his herculean efforts to establish his right as the heir. He consulted his lawyer who in turn, directed Nandi Varma to a leading lawyer in Rangoon who would straighten out things for him and help him fight for his rights. Nandi Varma went to Rangoon, met the lawyer and soon found himself hectically fighting for his right. The Rangoon Government posed a number of problems and tried its level best to prevent a foreigner from depleting its wealth, though he had the law on his side. After much wrangling Nandi Varma succeeded in his claim. Joyously he returned home with his well merited inheritance.

We, the individuals steeped in ignorance (avidyā), are Nandi Varmas. Buffeted by the storms of passions and tempests of desires, utterly exhausted, physically wrecked and emotionally spent, we come to a spiritual Master who is the repository of inexhaustible kindness. Just as Vishnu Varma said that Nandi was the heir of Shridhara Varma, so too, the spiritual teacher tells us that we are the Supreme. He tells us, 'That thou art.' Though we hear that we are the Supreme, we do not immediately become That. Mere knowledge that we are the Supreme does not elevate us to the pinnacle of Godhood. What we have heard objectively must become a subjective experience. Towards this end we ought to persevere, just as Nandi Varma fought tenaciously to establish his claim. We too, have to fight our way through, turning away from the ephemeral, and move towards the eternal. Surrendering ourselves to the Supreme and drawing inspiration from It, we ought to engage ourselves in overcoming the urges of the lower in us. This then, is the total integral sādhanā which should culminate in our intuitively experiencing the Supreme.

20. The Tiger's Mask

The sun was setting on the Western horizon, bathing the clouds in that region with an aura of crimson glow. The city of Madras seemed to be decked in a rosy garb. The red rays dancing on the waters of the river Cooum spread its crimson pall over the murky waters. Murugavel, who passed that way in his car, caught sight of the splendour of the setting sun. This sight overfilled his heart with calmness of the evening. As his car was manoeuvering a bend, his eye caught sight of an attractive colourful banner announcing the springing up of a new petrol bunk in that area. Then Murugavel remembered that it was the day of the week when his car had to be filled with gasoline. So he drove straight into the bunk. A uniformed attendant ran towards the car. Murugavel gave his keys to him and said, "25 litres!" The attendant took the keys, opened the tank, filled it with the desired quantity of petrol, closed the tank, returned the keys to Murugavel and checked the air pressure of the tyres. Receiving a hundred rupee note, he went into the bunk and returned with the receipt, the remaining change and a polythene packet as a gift. Murugavel received the packet, dumped it on the seat beside him, tipped the attendant and speeding, joined the concourse of cars on the road.

It was fifteen minutes later he reached his bungalow. Parking his car in the garage, he emerged out. It was then that he remembered he had left the polythene packet in the car itself. So once again he went into the garage and taking the gift began examining it. It was a gift packet with compliments from the new petrol bunk opened that day. The packet had a floral design on it. On it were also printed the name of the bunk in large print and that of the proprietor in small print. Driven by curiosity, he tore open the packet then and there itself and lo! Inside it he found a nice cardboard mask in black and yellow. It was the mask of a tiger. Elastic bands on either side of the mask invited him to give it a trial. He too felt a strange desire to try it on, unbecoming of his status and age; taking complete hold of him, lock, stock and barrel, to wear the mask of the tiger. So, using the elastic bands, he donned the mask and, peeking through the slots in it, made his way towards the house.

Murugavel's son, a tiny tot, hardly three summers old with toddling steps had just then come out. The father, in all love, roared, "Hey, sonny, look at me!" The child looked at the apparition and was beside himself with an unknown fear. Instantaneously he began to cry, weeping and wailing. Unwittingly, Murugavel in the tiger's mask had frightened the child. Yet he was not conscious of it. He began wondering why the child was wailing and weeping. The more he moved towards the child, the more he tried to console the child, the more uncontrollable became the child's wailing. The child's mother, who was busy preparing a special salad for the evening, hearing the sudden shriek of the child, picked up the biggest nearest ladle and rushed out to see what it was that had frightened her darling child. But when she came out to the portico, she saw her foolish husband, past forty, flaunting on his face the mask of a tiger. So, she burst forth, "Ay, you there, I thought you had evolved out of your childhood long back, but now I see that you are still childish. It ill becomes you to wear that mask. Do you not know that by wearing the mask you are not amusing the child but frightening him by displaying your unnatural self?" She took her child in her arms and wiping the hot tears that cascaded down the soft rosy cheeks, said, "Sonny, now look, I am here, you need not be afraid. The apparition there is not a tiger but your sweet daddy, it is only a mask that he is wearing. Look, now he has removed it". The child, who was in his twelfth wave of paroxysm slowly opened his eyes and, looked through the gap in his fingers. Then he saw his father with that abominable mask in his hands. Though his fear was now gone, the after-effects of his fear still continued to function through him. Gone was the mask and with it the abomination of otherness.

Spirit, functioning through the matter envelopments, is the living organism. 'That' dressed up in matter is the vainful 'Thou'. Therefore, man undressed of matter, is the eternal and the infinite Spirit. The scriptures say that all of us are Gods. But in our ignorance we come to wear the mask of the body, mind, intellect (BMI) and through it, look at the world and get deluded. Thus we come to frighten our ownselves on the other side. The scriptures ask us to put aside this mask of the BMI which is abominable and look at things as they are, as they ought to be. We are at present imperfect only because we identify ourselves with the body, mind and intellect. If only we refuse to see through this mask but look with the eyes of intuition, we will gain the vision divine.

21. The Businessman and The Rogue

Krishnalal had just then received a trunk call from Jayantilal of Madras. It was of an important nature, involving an investment of eight lakhs in a business deal out of which ultimately he would get a net profit of at least ten lakhs. If he let go this opportunity, perhaps never more would the goddess of fortune smile on him. So he decided to take the earliest opportunity of meeting Jayantilal of Madras. Krishnalal, by virtue of his extra dynamism and intellectual acumen, had established a network of business concerns in the Delhi complex. No doubt he was one of the noted black marketers. Now his greed to earn ten lakhs egged him on to book a ticket for himself to go to Madras. It was his trusted cashier who was sent to make reservation on the Grand Trunk Express to Madras, the following day.

As the cashier was busy at the reservation counter, a notorious rogue who was known to take on different manifestation in achieving his objective, and who had an eye on all the big businessmen who were on his list, happened to come to the ticket counter on one of his reconnoitering trips. The moment he saw the cashier, he accosted him and by his sweet behaviour, wormed out of the cashier the truth that Krishnalal was on his way to Madras to clinch a deal worth several lakhs. The rogue's mind began to work fast. Soon he had a plan up his sleeve. Only he waited for the cashier to leave the counter. Soon he too booked a berth for himself in the same compartment by which Krishnalal would travel.

The following day, Krishnalal boarded the train bound for Madras. The rogue too, in his best clothes, flaunting a diamond ring on his finger and a gold chain round his neck, got into the compartment. Luckily, his berth was opposite to that of Krishnalal's. Soon he introduced himself to Krishnalal as a businessman from Punjab on his way to Madras to attend the wedding of his uncle's son. He pretended to have business connections with various merchants, and talked in terms of lakhs and millions. Soon he seemed to gain Krishnalal's confidence by his glib and pleasant talk.

That night Krishnalal retired at 9 p.m itself. The rogue was reading the Picture Post. At 10.30 p.m., he lowered the magazine and observed that his co-traveller was fast asleep. Now he put his plan into action. He rummaged through Krishnalal's suitcase using his master key and searched his belongings thoroughly for the hard cash he had brought.

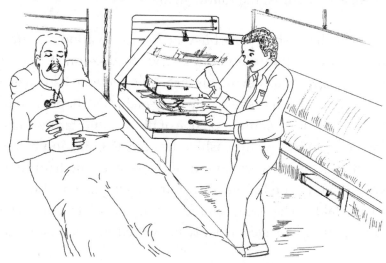

For all his deft search, he could not detect the hard cash. The bulging wallet Krishnalal had brought was also missing. 'Where could he have kept it'?, so mused the rogue. He was at his wit's end. He could not sleep well.

The next morning, when he returned from the toilet, to his dismay, he found the corpulent businessman counting his wad of notes! Lo! the wallet was on his lap. The day slowly wore off and turned into night again. The rogue decided to intensify the search. That night too, the businessman retired early. Giving him sufficient time to go into deep slumber, the rogue effected a thorough search. Everything except the wallet was there. A second time he went through the belongings of Krishnalal, but all was in vain, despite his leaving nothing unturned. The poignancy of his disappointment was all the more when this time too, he failed to trace the wallet and the wad of notes his eyes had so eagerly espied that morning. Never before in his life had his sagacity left him so cold.

In the early hours of the third morning when he returned from the toilet, as if to tease him, the businessman was gleefully counting the wad of notes. This time the wallet was by his side. Now the train was nearing Madras. When they alighted at Madras, Krishnalal thanked the rogue for giving him good company. The culprit too, returned the compliment. All the while thirsting to know where exactly the businessman had managed to hide the wallet during the nights. So he asked him outright about it. Krishnalal, with a broad grin, replied that he had been keeping the wallet every night right under the rogue's pillow!

We are the rogues, running eagerly after the world of objects, emotions and thoughts, searching for the hidden peace and an all enchanting bliss. We plod on and on endlessly, getting caught in the myriad mutabilities of samsāra and face disappointment repeatedly. The scriptures repeatedly tell us that the much sought after Bliss, the real peace, is right under our very noses. It is the very subject within us.

22. The Criminal and The President

The care and attention the middle class man in India bestows on his children is something remarkable. What with the spiralling prices, freezing wages and nagging taxes, he still finds time to take good care of his children. He wants his children to live well, learn deeply and thereby widen their horizon of knowledge. With this end in view, he keeps his children well-informed. Whenever he goes out, he takes with him his children. On all such occasions he describes to them all that he sees and hears and helps them understand it all. Evening walks, weekly outings, monthly retreats and quarterly excursions are a must for his kids; that is what a middle class man feels. So he strives, drudges and toils, willingly taking in his stride the overtime work offered to him. Thus he tries to earn well so that he can spend it justly and judiciously in the upbringing of his dear ones.

One such middle class man with his seven year old son was seen one day on a routine evening walk. Taking great pains he began explaining to his son how he could recognise the make of the cars that whizzed past them. Just then, a thick-lipped, dark skinned, heavily moustached, hefty young man in tight pants and a sportsman's shirt marched by them. Flanked on either side of this man were two constables, in full uniform, marching with their muskets. The hefty young man was in chains. The constables holding the chains were

121

marching forward. The very sight of this hefty young man struck terror in the hearts of the passers-by.

The seven year old, looking curiously at this man, asked his father, "Daddy, who is this young man?" The father said, "Sonny, this young man is a criminal, a delinquent and a malefactor, a transgressor. He is a murderer, an enemy of mankind. Left free, he will murder many, to whet his appetites and passions. So he is hounded out, caught', bound in chains and brought to book. He will be taken to the police station and remanded to custody. His case will be tried by a magistrate and due punishment will be given to him soon. These policemen flanking him are there to see that he does not escape. He cannot now run away, for he is in chains and the armed policemen are wary. The policemen are his escorts. They are there to guard him and conduct him to prison. They have full control over him now". The boy seemed to understand everything his father said. They walked on.

Now they came to a national highway, broad, tar topped and well kept. But there seemed to be no flow of traffic on this highway then. The father and the son were walking on one side of the road instead of on the pavement. A constable came running towards them and asked them to step on to the pavement. It was then that the father noticed that on either side of the road people had gathered in large numbers. Some had obtained, with great difficulty, vantage positions. From the balconies of the buildings on either side the expectant throng peeped & peered out. Minute by minute the throng seemed to surge. The observant father soon surmised that all this indicated that a high dignitary was on a state visit.

Perhaps he was to pass that way. The throng had come there to have a view of the august procession.

The middle class man, elbowing himself into the throng, managed to get enough room for him and his son to stand and watch from a vantage point. The gabble of the crowd was soon hushed, for there came just then, the cavalry pushing the crowd to the extreme edge of the road. Then came a police van hooting its siren. This was followed by a police lorry jam-packed with helmeted police. The Deputy Superintendent of Police was the next in the concourse. Then a cavalcade of traffic sergeants on their majestic motorcycles passed them. Then followed the cars flaunting their state flags, in which were seated the local ministers. Then a long, shining, open limousine slid past, and on its back seat was majestically seated the smiling President, dressed in white. On either side of the limousine and keeping pace with it, were the traffic sergeants on their two wheelers. Then a jeep passed in which were huddled the other dignitaries. In the rear of this majestic cavalcade came two police vans.

The boy, who was observing with gusto this grand procession, unable to contain his joy at having understood what it was all about, burst forth with the words, "Daddy, daddy, there goes the worst criminal on earth, heavily guarded." The bewildered father, muffling his son's mouth with his upper garment said, "Sonny, you are wrong. He is our President". The boy, pushing off the upper garment, said, "Well daddy, only an hour back you told me that if a man is flanked on either side by policemen, he is a criminal. Now I see that man in the limousine heavily flanked, guarded in front and rear by helmeted police and so I concluded that he must be the worst criminal". The conjunction of these two events, one parodying the other, made the father say, "No, sonny, he is our President, the first citizen of the nation. By virtue of his dedicated service, indefatigable industry and extraordinary merit, he has come to adorn the post of the President. So it is the nation's duty to honour, protect and

serve him. Further, he is the supreme commander of the forces of our nation. The Army, the Navy and the Air Force wait on him. They are at his beck and call. He is the supreme master. The President is the best of men. The criminal is the worst of mankind. The President, though flanked by policemen has full authority over them. They are there to serve, honour and revere him. They wait on him. The criminal in chains is ruled by the police. He is a slave in the hands of the police. The President is the master of the police, whereas the criminal is a slave of the police."

Thus ended the procession, so passed the evening, and so did the middle class man and his son.

This parable gives us an idea of the ocean of difference between a disciplined seeker and an undisciplined one. He who keeps his intellect pure and well-informed, his mind in restraint and control, guiding his life on the path of the good without allowing his senses to run wild, down the embankments into the muddy fields of reckless pleasures, is a wise man. He comes to live a happy, blissful and rapturous life like the President. But he who is a slave of the senses is like the criminal. He allows his mind and senses to run loose, and naturally the unruly senses, wild and mad as they are unleashed, go dashing and wrecking him on the roadside of life. He falls on the scale of evolution and reaches the lowest state of animal existence, for he fails to keep an intelligent self-control on his own endless sense demands.

23. Beware of The Hunter

The finest species of fowl are found in the dense jungles of Daṇḍaka forest. It is a feast for the eyes to see the birds coming in groups of twenties to thirties to roost in the trees with verdant foliage. Many an ornithologist has wended his way to this forest with the main object of studying the birds in this locality. Into this forest once did trek an anchorite, young in years, strong in build and kind of heart. The birds there shared their happiness with the anchorite by pouring into his enraptured ears their lilting notes of lovesome music. On such occasions the anchorite would get absorbed in the melody with which God had blessed these birds. Many were the species of birds had their habitat in the lush foliage of the dense jungle. The anchorite often lost himself in thought, admiring the happy life of artless kind of the fowls there.

Once, as he was passing that way, much to his chagrin he saw, a sturdy hunter greedily eyeing the fowls perched atop the trees. The anchorite's curiosity was aroused, for the hunter had neither a bow nor any arrows with him. But on his back was a huge net and a basket slung at his side. When he saw the concourse of birds, his eyes began to sparkle. Soon, he scattered some grain, spread the net and waited at some distance. The birds in the trees, seeing the grains scattered on the ground, flew down, alighted on the ground and began to peck at them. Alas! they were soon trapped in the tangle of the net. The hunter lifted the net which now contained the wealth of birds. Heaving them on to his head he carried it to the city to make a fortune out of them. The anchorite who was espying all this, was sad at heart at the fate of the birds. He felt that he should warn the species against the hunter. He thought that he should do that good turn then itself. So he went back into the dense jungle and looking up at the birds that still remained there and said, "Blessed fowls of the air, pray pay heed to what I say. There is a hunter who visits this forest daily. He is your enemy, for he is bent on decimating your population. Everyday he comes here, tempts you into his net and carries away with him a large flight of your kind. Hence remember, the hunter will come, he will scatter the grain and spread the net, you will peck at the seeds and get trapped. So, beware of the hunter! Beware of the hunter!" Then, after a pause, he said, "Birds, do you understand what I say?" The birds said in unison, "Yes, yes, we do understand what you say". The anchorite who wanted to make sure that the birds had understood the message well, said, "If that be so, please repeat what I said". Immediately, the birds sang in a chorus. "Beware of the hunter! Beware of the hunter!" When the anchorite heard this, he was beside himself with joy. Now he was sure that the birds would not fall prey to the machinations of the vile hunter. As he was going away from that place, he could hear them chirping in chorus, "The hunter will come. Beware of the hunter! Beware of the hunter!"

The next day the hunter, greedy as he was, wanted to trap a large number of birds and so had come with a bigger net. But just as he was about to scatter the grain, he was

surprised to hear the birds chirping, as if it were a nursery rhyme, the subject matter of which shocked him beyond his wits. He heard the words, 'The hunter will come, he will scatter the grain and spread the net. We will peck at them and get trapped. So beware of the hunter! Beware of the hunter!' The puzzled hunter, on hearing these words threw down his basket of grain and the net in a vexatious mood. Overcome with exhaustion caused by despair, he relaxed his aching limbs and soon mother sleep enveloped him.

After an hour, when the hunter awoke, a surprise awaited him. Contrary to his expectations, he saw his net sagging with the weight of the fowls. The surprise was all the more so, because the fowl inside the net were still repeating. 'The hunter will come, he will scatter the seeds and spread the net and we will get caught. So beware of the hunter! Beware of the hunter!' The hunter, laughed to his heart's content on hearing this cackle of the foolish birds. Lifting the net full of his booty, he happily flitted through the forest on his onward march to the market.

The anchorite who came that way again, saw to his surprise, the hunter and his booty. He was dismayed that the birds, oblivious of their lot, were still foolishly chirping in chorus. "Beware of the hunter! Beware of the hunter!" The anchorite said to himself, 'Now I see the truth. Mere repetition of the advice without understanding the significance of it, is of no avail'.

We too, in this world, many a time act foolishly just like the birds. We go on chanting and repeating mechanically many a words of wisdom without a thought to its significance or meaning and hence fail to reap the benefit of these chants and verses.

24. Be A Light Unto Thyself

In the sequestered valleys of the mighty mountain ranges of the snow-capped Himalayas, there live, even to this day, a sacred order of sannyāsins spending their time in study, reflection and meditation, restraining their senses, regulating their reflexes and leading the mind into transcendental heights. The atmosphere there is conducive to lift their minds to infinite dimensions. The very valleys reverberate with and echo the sacred chants and divine hymns, sung by the devout anchorites in a measured sequence, rich in mellifluous melody.

Not a day passes for these anchorites without their ever chanting the Vedas or without their ever participating in the lively satsangas[1] in these idyllic settings. Each and every one of these sannyāsins has his simple abode in the sheltered cottages situated on the verdurous slopes of the valleys. Everyday they all meet at a central place, usually a common hermitage, where they have their lively satsangas. The older ones share their subtle experiences with the younger ones, who in turn, lend charm and grace to the very place. On all sunny days, these aspirants, seekers, anchorites and sannyāsins converge to that central place to draw as much inspiration as they can. With pure minds and warm hearts they come under the benign influence of the holy atmosphere prevailing in that place.

[1] Satsanga - discussions with wisemen of God

Though these satsaṅgas generally continue till late in the evenings, it is not uncommon for them sometimes, to end the satsaṅgas abruptly. Such a contingency arises only by the occurrence of a special phenomenon, not uncommon in these parts. Suddenly the valley will clothe itself in utter darkness and there will be no light until dawn. On such occasions the participants disperse and adjourn to their huts, with fond hopes of assembling the next day. To these lovely satsaṅgas sometimes there comes, from one of the slopes, an old saint bent double with age. He was born blind. The anchorites and the sannyāsins in the valley look tenderly upon him and often help him back to his hut after the satsaṅga concludes. On some days the old blind saint prefers to go alone to his hut.

On one such occasion, as the satsaṅga was in progress, darkness suddenly swept in and the session had to conclude abruptly. The blind old sannyasin was struggling. One of the

anchorites taking pity on the sore distress of the old sannyasin helped him get up, and giving him his walking stick, placed in his hand a coconut pail. Then putting a candle in it, he lighted it. The blind sannyāsin asked the anchorite what he was doing. In all love the anchorite said, "Mahārāja, do you not know it has grown dark? So I am giving you a coconut shell with a lighted candle in it". The blind sannyāsin said with a chuckle, "Arey, buddhu! (Ay, fool) Do you not know that I am as blind as an owl? Even in broad daylight I cannot see anything, so how can I see anything with this little candle light?" Pat came the reply, "Hey Mahārāja, do I not know you are blind? This candlelight is not to help you see, but to help others see you, so that in the darkness others may not bump into you and trip you down". Then the satisfied sannyāsin said, "Ha! Ha! Is that so? Then let me hold it firmly and move slowly. May Nārāyaṇa bless you for your kind gesture!" The anchorite put the old saint in the right direction. Tip... tap... tip... tap ... ! The blind man started walking back to his hut feeling every step with his stick. All the while he was holding the coconut shell carefully in his palm.

The sannyāsin's hut was in the thickest part of the jungle, and now the foliage intensified the darkness. As the sannyāsin was nearing his hut, a man emerging from darkness bumped into him and as a result, the blind man tripped. Yet he held the coconut shell tightly in his palm. The man who had bumped into him, lifted the old sannyāsin up, and apologetically said, "Mahārāja, please pardon me. Are you all right, Mahārāja? In the gathering darkness I did not see you coming. Had I any inkling of your approach, I would not have stumbled against you. Please excuse me. Shall I guide you to your hut?" The irate sannyāsin with all vehemence said, "You fool, did you not see the lighted candle in my hand? Are you blind? Seeing the lighted candle, you could have desisted from bumping into me. You have the audacity to say that it is all dark. Look! Look! I have in my palm a lighted candle!" So saying, he held the coconut shell up for the intruder to observe. The intruder saw no light, and so concluded that the sannyāsin was tipsy, but saying nothing in reply, quickly went away from the place.

What had actually happened was that as the sannyāsin was entering the thickest part of the jungle, a passing breeze had put out the candlelight. The sannyāsin being blind could not notice it. Hence he blamed the man who bumped into him as he expected the man to notice the lighted candle in his hand, little conscious of the fact that the light had been put out long before he met the man.

In the field of spirituality, many a seeker come to a Realised Master. The Master in turn instructs, guides and shapes the student and makes him gain glimpses of the Truth. The teacher lights the candle of knowledge in the heart of the seeker and then sends him out into the field of work to preach to the multitude about the might and majesty of the Lord. The seekers are advised to keep their lights burning. What keeps the light burning in the seeker is his sādhanā.[1] When the seeker becomes slack in his sādhanā, the light goes out. Through study, reflection and meditation, he should trim his light and keep it burning. He

---

[1] sādhanā - the spiritual practices required to reach Godhood.

must be a light unto others. When a seeker comes out into the field, if there is no sufficient sādhanā, the audience do not recognise any worth in him. But the seeker, imagining that the light of knowledge is still burning in him, demands reverence and respect from the audience! The teacher's instructions to him are, 'Keep the light burning. If the light is put out, through sādhanā light it up again. Be a light unto yourself and to others. Lag not in your sādhanā. Śravaṇa (listening) manana (reflection) and nididhyāsana (meditation) are necessary practices needed to light you up.'

25. Precept and Practice

John of Lovedale was an exceptionally good man. Polished in manners, spruce in habiliments, tidy in upkeep and trim in his transactions with others, he was honoured and respected everywhere. Blessed with a moderate intelligence, he could speculate fairly easily and follow dexterously the trends of the bulls and bears in the stock exchange. Fortune smiled on him at the right time and he found himself inheriting a decent property from a distant relative of his. This inheritance enabled him to establish a grocery shop of his own, in a busy locality of Lovedale. The commodities he sold were of decent kind and he, on his part, gave his customers rich satisfaction, for, 'consumer service' was his watchword. His business prospered and this enabled him to buy off, in a lean period, a cosy apartment at a stone's throw from his thriving business shop, which teemed with activity all the time. Dull would be the life for any person if it has no ups and downs. Margaret was one of his customers. She had youth and pretty beauty, which had the simple charm and the delicate vigour of a wild flower. Immensely touched by the tenderness of the angelic Margaret, he began to woo her, and she too, found in him a kindness surpassing all description, and so she reciprocated his love. So the wooing culminated in a wedding. This gave immense satisfaction to John.

This happy-go-lucky John soon developed peculiar psychic trouble. This is how the trouble found its way into the mental structure of jolly John. The day after he moved to his new apartment, he found, midway between his apartment and the business store, a poultry. Poultry was the one thing he did not like in life. He was allergic even to hear of a poultry. When even to hear that word was anathema and allergy to him, how could he be at peace with himself when he had to pass by the poultry every time he went up or down to his shop? One might as well ask what gave John the creeps in his lumbar region. Well, it was the crowing of the cock in the poultry that sent him into tantrums of terrific unrest. Whenever he heard the 'cock-ro-kho-kho' of the cock he felt as if he were a worm chased by the cock with his sharp beak. He was mortally afraid that the cock would peck at him and make mincemeat of him. Try as he could, he was unable to overcome the sensation and feeling that he was a worm. He had this feeling only when he thought of the cock. A lion or a tiger he could face bravely, but a hen or a cock was a monster striking death and disaster in the innermost core of his shivering self.

Margaret, his lovesome wife, with whom he shared the joys of his life, soon discovered this peculiar slant in his behaviour and with many a kind word of advice, tried to bring sense into his mind that the cock was far smaller in size and stature than his own self, and hence, it did not have even a ghost of a chance to peck at him, much less to tear him to pieces. But, just as certain sentiments develop roots in one's personality and are hard to eradicate, so too, this feeling that he was a worm in the presence of the cock took strong hold of his mind and was eating his mind gradually. He grew thin and lanky. A famished look began permanently to inhabit his face. He lost all appetite for life. Margaret, pitying her husband's condition, soon convinced him that he should consult a psychiatrist.

A day was fixed and the day did come when John was moved to the famous medical complex in the heart of Lovedale, where the psychiatrist had with him the latest gadgets with which he could unearth and apprehend even the most subtle tendencies lying deep down in the abysmal depths of the subtle unconsciousness. Margaret too, entrusting the charge of running their shop to her sister, went with her husband to be a tower of strength to him when he was to be examined by the team of psychiatrists. The examination was a tedious one involving several tests. The last test was of a subtle kind where John was sent into a state of suspended animation. John was lying prostrate on the bed. A bright ray of light was focussed on the layers of his brain. Moving a sharp needle smoothly over the layers of the brain, the psychiatrist in a dreamy voice began addressing John. John too, responded in a voice, which appeared to come from a grave. The doctor was satisfied with the test. He had diagnosed the disease correctly. He started treating the patient with right medicines. In three days John was cured of his complaint. He felt all right. Now he was full of confidence that he was not a worm and that the cock could do nothing to him. The next day he was discharged.

John was all smiles that day. Margaret was in all bloom. The two appeared like a happy couple who had just then walked out of the garden of Eden. Paying all the bills, thanking the doctors profusely, the two came out, happily humming a happy tune. That being a pleasant day, a sunny morning with all the pleasantness of spring, they decided to walk the distance between the hospital and their apartment. They had hardly gone a couple of hundred metres, when a cock somewhere in the locality, for no reason, began to crow 'cock-ro-kho-kho' at that odd hour. This crowing of the cock stung John to the quick, and without even telling Margaret, he ran so fast back to the hospital that, had a sprinters' race been held then, he would have hit the tape first! Margaret, who least expected such a thing to happen, ran after John to the hospital. When she reached the hospital, she could hear John asking the very psychiatrist who had treated him, "Doctor, I know very well that I am not a worm to be pecked at by the cock, but does the cock know I am not a worm? ! What would happen to me if he should still think that I am a worm?" The psychiatrist and Margaret were flabbergasted. It was at that juncture that I left the three of them in the hospital, two of them with mouths opened wide, eyes bulging out, a picture of dismay staring at John.

Though John's condition is funny, most of us in this world are no better than John. Knowledge we have accumulated in plenty. But when it is a question of using it in a situation, we find that this knowledge leaves us high and dry. However much one may read and understand anything, if it is not assimilated into one's own personality to become a deep rooted conviction in oneself, that individual's condition is no better than John's.